Praise for Foreignpreneur

*B*efore you start a business, read this book!

"Foreignpreneur® gives you insight into the real-life of an entrepreneur and provides you the opportunity to learn from personal stories. It will prevent you from falling into the trap of the typical entrepreneur stories all over the internet, which doesn't show you the fundamentals of building a business, but rather, how cool it is to live a luxury life as a CEO. This book is a must-read before you hit roadblocks, which can be eliminated if you were aware of the information that's given to you in this book!"— ***Samir Huseynzade (Application Developer at ExxonMobil)***

"Vibrant, educative, and motivating read! Every phase of the generic path of a foreign entrepreneur is captured; from first steps to hits and misses, as well as scaling up success!" — ***Obinna Nwachukwu (Automotive Engineer at Bosch Magyarország & TEDx Speaker)***

"Very useful information for anyone who has a dream to be an entrepreneur, especially in a different country. There are all sorts of pitfalls and problems you could encounter. This book provides real useful tips, suggestions, and processes to make that dream happen. Highly recommended." —*Michele Berner (Chief Editor, Foreignpreneur®)*

"I have spent a lot of time with Davies and have been amazed by his incredible insights in business, coupled with his experiences. *Foreignpreneur* explicitly identifies nine dependencies that play a key part in starting and running a successful business as a foreigner. If you are serious about strategically positioning your business for success, don't just read this book - note the dependencies and approach them strategically." —*Anthony C. Ejiogu, Speaker, Creator of The Success Elite*

Foreignpreneur provides a very practical guide on how to contemplate, conceive, implement and succeed at doing business in a foreign country. The author, Davies Iyiegbu has successfully created a book that can be likened to, 'starting a business as a foreign entrepreneur for dummies'. It is an elegant and gallant approach. I recommend it." — **H.E Dr. Eniola Ajayi Ambassador of the Federal Republic of Nigeria to Hungary**

"This book was written in everyday language, no vocabulary twists, just your average guy next door. Take your time to go through every reflective quote and relate it to either yourself or someone you know."

FOREIGNPRENEUR®

The 9 Dependencies of Success & *How to Think Like a Foreign Entrepreneur*: What you need to start an international or small business

DAVIES IYIEGBU

Copyright © 2017 by Davies Iyiegbu. All rights reserved.

ISBN: 978-978-973-344-6

The views expressed in this book are personal views and may not be scientifically proven; readers consent to understand this and does not hold the author liable.

Questions can be sent by email author@foreignpreneur.net or visit www.foreignpreneur.net.
Follow the Foreignpreneur pages: Facebook: www.facebook.com/foreignpreneur.
Twitter: @Foreignpreneur
Instagram: @Foreignpreneur

Acknowledgment

I will like to acknowledge the effort of all those who contributed to this book in various ways. Everyone who read this book when it was unreadable, submitted their thoughts about the readability, cover designs, editing, and forewords.

Michele Berner, Unah Henry, Ali Bayramli, Farkas Greta, Tony-Bruno Izuchkwu, Faith Abang, Khezami Kholoud, Sabathy Us, Emmanuel Ahiafor, Ngure Rainette,Obianuju Unegbu, Anthony Ejiogu, Stephen Okoye, Precious Iyiegbu, Alfreda Iyiegbu.

To my family. My dear wife, Adrienn Iyiegbu-Szabo, my lovely daughter, Naila Iyiegbu-Szabo, who inspired me to keep writing, even when the motivation was drained. You all made this significant task, seem easy but it wasn't. Here we are, the writing is complete, and the reading has started.

Thank you,

Davies Iyiegbu

Author.

Contents

Preface

*M*ost of the time, the mindset of a foreign entrepreneur is preoccupied with perfecting the art of being successful, attending conferences, reading books, finding all sorts of inspirational quotes that drive up their ego to be self-employed. They are easily swayed by the *"become your own boss"* tagline which only scratch the surface of how hard it is to build a business abroad.

They are easily fascinated by the success stories of Mark Zuckerberg building a social media company from a dorm room or Steve Jobs building one of the world's most valuable company from a garage, but they forget to ask, *where are the stories of their sleepless nights?* Their journeys. How did they manage to be a father and an entrepreneur? Moreover, how did they find the perfect work-life balance? Did they deal with debts? Manage investor tantrums and built partnerships?

Of course, these stories always come out as autobiography books, years after the entrepreneur is at the end of his or her career. If entrepreneurs feel the need to read books, which leaves them with a continuous desire to be like their mentor, then they need to see beyond the fantasy success stories of their mentor(s) and dive deep into how their mentor(s) dealt with all the interwoven factors and challenges that made them successful at what they do.

There is a need to tell the real entrepreneurship stories for young entrepreneurs to understand the real struggles and walk their path in reality and not in fantasies. This enables the society to have more long-lasting economic growth through jobs and wealth created by these entrepreneurs and not the other way round —when young entrepreneurs are aspiring to get to unattainable heights and standards set by untrue stories of rag to riches— what that creates; is an *"Avalanche of depressed CEOs, a society-inflicted chaos of mental issues for failed entrepreneurs."*

In pursuit of my entrepreneurial path, I have learnt to set expectations. Expectations come with anxiety and anticipation. If you control both, then you don't get booted by —disappointment.

In all my years of being an entrepreneur, I kept looking for an answer to this question.

"Why am I successful and not another person who has given it, the same effort as me?"

When I look back through the struggles and hustles, there were certain times when I would wonder if my wife understood why I stayed long hours at work and forgot to send her a happy birthday message. This could have simply led to a divorce that can affect my mental focus and aspects of my life and business, the result? Failure.

I reckon that we all work hard at some point in our lives pursuing our dreams and sometimes, I thought that my family's support was the sole reason for my successes. Other times, I thought it was the country I chose to live and do business. Sometimes, I thought it was my luck, network, education, or business partners. The list keeps growing as I keep searching for the answers to what my success depends on.

The same goes to those realistic thoughts of; perhaps I could have failed if I did not secure that all-important meeting or lucky enough to have been in that networking conference at the right time to meet the right people.

Then, I realized that I could not single out any one of these factors because every single one of them was instrumental and contributed to my success, and was equally as important as the other.

Every moment mattered, and each of those moments came together to create a significant moment of success. I realized that it is a process and not a trophy, and I began to think:

"Process over trophy."

As an entrepreneur, you need to be aware of what your success depends on and be able to navigate your path by controlling and managing those dependencies. Because, in the unwritten rules of success, there is no secret to success, neither is there that one path to being successful.

In the next chapters of this book, we will discuss the nine dependencies that every foreign entrepreneur should be aware of; in theory, personal experience and how to approach each of the dependencies.

I call them the nine building blocks of a foreign entrepreneur. These dependencies may have overlapping connotations or meanings with those of an entrepreneur, but a foreign entrepreneur should be aware of all nine dependencies to be able to build a successful business in a different society or outside their country.

Introduction

*I*n 2012, online advertising was booming, targeting web and mobile surfers. Mobile penetration was on a steady rise. *Google* had just introduced *Google AdSense*, a service that connects advertisers to bloggers, and on the other hand, web, and app developers could place an advertisement on their website to earn a fee per click.

As the growth sprung to record heights, there was extensive criticism of this type of advertising due to data privacy concerns. Users were getting increasingly frustrated with pop up ads interrupting their video streaming or web browsing experience. A situation that is still persistent today.

In the wild busy streets somewhere in Africa, a young boy thought to himself, why not come up with an alternative advertising solution that will reach the same target audience as Google AdSense but less aggressive with zero privacy concerns? So, he came up with an idea to place third-party advertising on a mobile recharge card printed by telecommunications companies and their retail agents nationwide. A market that encompasses over hundred and thirteen million active phone subscribers.

His idea would give value to disposable mobile recharge cards known as mobile top-up cards used to credit mobile phones across the streets in most African cities. The boy quickly turned on his worn-out Veda laptop computer, downloaded Photoshop graphics software and started designing models of how to make advertising possible on pieces of disposable paper.

While he succeeded in putting together a design and sample proposal, he realized there was still more work to be done. Now he had to figure out how to get an appointment in one of the biggest telecommunication companies in Africa, a very uphill task in a society where almost everything is based on connections and knowing people who know the powers that be. However, nothing was going to deter him from achieving his dream of disrupting the advertising industry.

So, he borrowed a few bucks from his dad and purchased fuel from roadside buyers on hot sunny days to get to the busy high-end areas where most companies had their corporate offices.

It was just the beginning of his entrepreneurship journey. At this point in his mission, the only thing he had considered was *"I am going to be successful by any means necessary."* He was overwhelmed in making sure that his dream of changing the advertising industry was not going to go away quickly.

As he managed to find his way into the office of — one of Africa's most significant domestic telecommunication company without an appointment, it was apparent his name was not on the visitor's list.

The security immediately yelled, *"Who are you looking for?"* The boy took a deep breath as he realized he had just encountered his first entrepreneurship challenge, *"Self Confidence."* —*"I have a proposal for your company, and I think your marketing manager would love to see this.* "The boy responded.

The security personnel asked for a copy of the proposal, and scanned through the paper, his cheeks slowly expanded as he smiled at the boy and said: *"You need to see the marketing manager."*

The boy had passed his first test and was ushered in to meet the marketing manager. In the meeting with the manager, he went on to explain his idea with passion and enthusiasm. He received a positive feedback and an invitation to come back to do a proper presentation.

Negotiations continued between the boy and the telecommunication company, but this would soon be his first setback in his entrepreneurship journey as he hit the voicemail of the marketing manager more times than it actually took him to write the proposal.

The last straw was when he discovered that a copy of his idea had been released for electioneering campaigns without his consent.

He slowly began to realize that the journey to stardom would be a hard one. He proceeded to file a lawsuit (see Appendix B) and came up with a couple of more innovative ideas with each ending the same way. Then the boy thought to himself, why not travel abroad to further his studies and continue his entrepreneurship dreams? At least he could see how advanced countries such as the United States and the European continent encourage the startup culture.

So, he dusted off his computer degree, stored in a cupboard that he'd barely opened months after his graduation, and started searching the internet for universities in Europe. It took him hours to weeks trying to find the cheapest and the best universities. A correlation that is very hard to find.

Because, of course, the cheapest things are usually not associated with the best, and the best is always the most expensive.

He finally got tired of searching and decides to phone a friend who studies in one of the central European countries; his friend helped provide him with the information he needed to make a choice and soon he was admitted into the same university as his friend.

Admission secured, the dream seemed within reach; why not? The boy proceeded to board a Lufthansa Boeing 737 airplane to central Europe. His thoughts often ran wild on how his idea would be a significant success in Europe, and he could approach a few companies and get a bunch of interested investors. On landing at Frankfurt airport, the first stopover for a connecting flight to his final destination, he would get the first glimpse of Europe as he quickly felt the cold breeze of Frankfurt, Germany.

He immediately realized how far away from home he was and his first thought was to call home, *so* he scanned the entire airport, looking for an international mobile recharge card. At least the boy knew what recharge cards were, since his mobile recharge card advertising idea was still his major accomplishment at the time.

On getting to the phone store, he asked, *"Please can I have a mobile recharge card?"* He was passed a point of sale (POS) machine, to recharge an existing compatible line or get a new sim card and the boy was amazed. He thought that almost every part of the world was still using mobile disposable recharge cards. So he quickly left the terminal to board the flight to his final destination.

However, deep in his mind, he was overwhelmed by the advancement in technology compared to where he was coming from. As he soliloquized, crazy thoughts kept flying in. *What more can I see along this journey?*

His destination was one hour, thirty minutes away from Frankfurt airport. So he decided to chill with movies and a bottle of drink. He kept up hope that he would find an alternative business model in Europe. As the boy landed and stepped out to the exit terminal of his destination airport, he tried to top-up his cell phone once more and was quickly greeted with similar technologies that he'd already seen at the Frankfurt airport.

His journey of becoming an entrepreneur was taking a new turn; he had gradually crossed the thin line of calling himself an entrepreneur to becoming a foreign entrepreneur. He would soon discover that the people were different, the food, the etiquette, economy as well as the technologies. The boy now had to quickly pick a new business, come up with a viable business model and, at the same time, start learning the new culture, the language, the people, the regulations and laws that govern the new city and country he would soon call home.

On a sunny Saturday, the boy took a walk to the park, remembering the difficulties he had experienced throughout the process of securing his university admission to study abroad. He has since begun to settle into the new city.

Reminiscent of all the struggles of a student visa, securing accommodation, travel insurance and transporting his forty-seven kg luggage from the airport to the student hostel, he had little or no knowledge about currency exchange, where to go and whom to ask. An experience he wished he never had to go through.

At this point, he decided that no other international student should experience the same difficulty as he had and from this experience, the boy decided to develop a university admission and travel mobile application for international students. This would make it easy for international students who want to study abroad to easily access university, travel and visa information via the app.

The app quickly became an instant success with thousands of downloads, and university partnerships were soon on the cards. Many of his friends who had similar dreams to study abroad just like him kept contacting the boy to get study abroad information. The search engines website, the first go-to place for most international students seeking to find information to study abroad, has the bulk of both relevant and irrelevant information, but it was difficult to filter or process easily. They needed an insider's perspective.

His friends wanted to know how long the visas would take, student jobs, university reputation, cost of living and country values. These were some of the few questions he was asked. The boy instantly knew he had something great, but the journey and the story were far from reality. Then came expansion; he needed to form a team, fund the business, and maintain a social life. Even though he had made his first step in becoming a foreign entrepreneur; he'd picked a new country and developed a business model; he still had no idea how to deal with culture, partnerships, funding, maintaining relationships with friends, family, and legal documentation.

Obviously to him, at this point, it was clear the entrepreneurship journey was a tough and lonely path — he had to figure out the answers to all these questions himself.

It then completely dawned on him that even though he had challenges starting up his business while back in Africa, he'd barely thought about cultural differences, funding, maintaining relationships with family & friends, legal papers and several other factors that his success as a foreign entrepreneur would depend on.

Two years down the road, as easy as these factors sounded in his subconscious mind, they would become the main reason for his first major business failure. Cultural differences in email communications, simple etiquette such as meeting timing, access to loans and grants, and maintaining his personal relationships would all become daunting tasks. Business deals were lost in language translations, and simple disagreements would often end in tantrums and arguments as failure began to look more like his best friend.

As he slowly got to his break point of fantasy and into the reality of what being a foreign entrepreneur entails, he took time off to go back to the drawing board to get a bigger picture of what being a foreign entrepreneur meant and to come up with a map for his journey to becoming successful.

Today, that boy from Africa is me, Davies Chigozie Iyiegbu (Nigerian), the founder of Study in Europe and Study in Budapest mobile apps, managing director of Goziex Technologies Limited and exclusive importer of the prestigious *Torley* brand in Nigeria; Hungary's oldest and largest winemaker with over 135 years of history in winemaking.

I am now married with a daughter, an IT project change management lead in one of the largest, fortune 500 energy companies in the world and living in Budapest, Hungary. The country of the hero square.

I have since moved on to organize the first technology-based fair in Nigeria with Budapest Metropolitan university, as an alumnus, to allow students to get on-the-spot admission just by using a mobile application with access to over fifteen thousand audiences.

It became the bedrock for the growth from a startup to an international company that solves problems for thousands of students and universities.

This book will look to narrate some of my challenges during my journey to becoming a successful foreign entrepreneur, what I have learnt and am still learning along this unending journey.

This book is ideal for startup founders, entrepreneurs, both those living abroad and in their local countries, anyone who intends to think like a foreign entrepreneur or someone who wants to start a business or motivate themselves from the stories of others.

After reading this book, you should be able to pick a business in or from a foreign country and strive to make it successful.

Chapter One

Meet a Foreignpreneur

Understanding the 9 Dependencies of Every Foreignpreneur

Have you ever found yourself in a situation where no one understands you and what you stand for? It is absolutely fine to feel different from your society. Most successful entrepreneurs are foreigners of their societal norms and old ways of doing things.

They strive to ask the **"Why?"** *question.*

They are curious about the **"How?"** and **"What?"** of already existing processes and norms. They consistently question the **"I"** in the **"We,"** and they strive to carve out the **"I"** *by* finding solutions to problems that everyone shares but most are not aware of.

"Most entrepreneurs often do not realize their uniqueness and their challenges until they fail."

Failure and challenges connect the dots for an entrepreneur and often make him, or her realize how foreign he or she is to the society they live in and most importantly, how the heck it is challenging to build a business from ground zero to a billion-dollar company. Until they fail, they always assume they are the next Mark Zuckerberg.

If you cannot sell an idea to a new society or convince your immediate community to buy a product or offer them a service, then you've just about started your first step in being a ***"Foreignpreneur."*** A Foreignpreneur means a *foreign entrepreneur or an individual who owns or aspires to own a business in a new society where the culture, the people, the language and environment is different from what that individual is accustomed to.*

"When a society does not understand the entrepreneur, they often do not buy the idea."

In 2012, as I mentioned in the introduction of this book, I developed my first valuable idea which I called the best idea of the 21st century; well at least that's what I would like to believe.

As an entrepreneur, you often think of yourself as a standout from the crowd and so for every "NO" someone says to your idea, there perhaps has to be another person who does not understand how the heck you want to change the world.

However, back to the story, grab your popcorn. As the sound of the Boeing airplane engine roared in my ear as it plundered into the high blue sky, tearing through the cloud on that sunny day in September of 2013, it was as if my desire to be a successful entrepreneur abroad was louder than the two engines combined. Then again, I had one setback in the mirror; the other side of me wanted to be a professional footballer. I was caught up in a paradox of choice of being a Jack of all trades.

I never realized how difficult growing a business as a foreign entrepreneur would be and neither did I have the slightest clue how hard being a professional footballer could be. I only had my bag, a few other valuable items and an admission letter to a university.

How that story changed from uncertainty to near certainty was my ability to realize the unique situations and challenges that I found myself in. I was able to quickly come up with an alternative business idea and an entirely new business model as soon as I realized that the society that I have since —moved to in Budapest, Hungary has adopted a more advanced technological way of recharging mobile phones: through POS machines, software-as-a-service (SaaS), and metro stores. This meant my *"best idea of the 21ˢᵗ century"* in Nigeria had just become a *1908 BC* idea in Budapest.

I had no doubt that finding a solution to the admission and travel problem that has faced millions of international students seeking to study abroad wasn't such a bad idea either and would be a perfect alternative. At the time, to think that I was able to do it successfully as a foreign entrepreneur meant that I was able to find and am still finding answers to all the dependencies that my success relied on.

> ***"They say a journey of a thousand miles starts with a step? However, you weren't told which step is the right step."***

I had no choice but to start re-thinking about other applications of my idea in Budapest. I had to find new ways to provide solutions to already existing problems in a different society which I now live in, but that wouldn't happen like magic. Changing a business model or an idea you are already comfortable with feels like changing the world.

Then comes the part where you not only have to convince the locals that you have the capacity to deliver value and solutions to an existing problem, but you also have to find that unique idea and business model that is scalable in your new society, while also keeping in mind your ability to manage new life events that will emanate from a new culture, new market, regulations, and goals.

Forty-four percent of Silicon Valley startups have foreign entrepreneurs as their founders. Fifty-one percent of startups worth a billion dollars was founded by foreign entrepreneurs; however, most of these foreign entrepreneurs had to overcome humongous regulations and roadblocks to build a successful business. Most countries still do not have regulations to integrate foreign entrepreneurs, for example, the United States still have no category for a startup visa, and startup founders have traditionally found it difficult to come and stay in the United States, and this is a peculiar situation in most countries. Openness to foreigners is one of the cultural values that predict future— economic growth on a city-by-city basis. [1]

The sheer number of challenges that a foreign entrepreneur has to overcome daily is enormous, from the simple question ***"Where are you from?"*** that you get in business meetings, which often knocks you off balance. Simply because you are not sure if your country is on the blacklist of your potential business partner to finding your way through the stringent regulations that segregate the citizens of the country you live in and your native country.

It is matter-of-factly a grey area that not many people consider as unique challenges, but foreign entrepreneurs have accepted this as part of their professional life, and nothing derails an entrepreneur more than his inability to spot difficulties before they come, even though you may wish to learn from your failure. However, it is better to avoid failure if you have the chance than to fail and pick yourself back up each time because:

"Not every failed entrepreneur gets a second chance."

Although, most investors will take a shot at a foreign founder or CEO who possess an incredible entrepreneurial trait. However, without the founder's ability to adapt to the new society and challenges that come with being a foreign —entrepreneur, that uniqueness which comes from the strength in diversity can quickly turn to one of those stories of beautiful ideas that end up in the cemetery.

The reality is that the most funded companies are not the most successful companies. It is a combination of the ability of the founder to scale the idea, put together a good team, manage life events and wiggle through the rigorous dependencies that make up the block to building a profitable business.

A foreign entrepreneur's initial mindset is that of success, with little or no concentration on the connection between his or her life events and the bits and pieces of the dependencies that will need to come together for him or her to be able to succeed in doing business in a foreign country.

From the vast experience which I have garnered in my years as a foreign entrepreneur and almost a decade as an entrepreneur, I was able to narrow down these challenges that I faced into nine main dependencies which I call the ***Foreignpreneur® Reality Model***.

The *Foreignpreneur® Reality Model* analyses the nine main challenges that either make or break a foreign entrepreneur. These are the nine building blocks of a successful foreign entrepreneur, and this model provides a visual representation and a set of techniques that a foreign entrepreneur can utilize to mitigate or maneuver through the hurdles of building a business in a new society.

The nine dependencies listed in the *Foreignpreneur® Reality Model* may be put into effect in a non-chronological order. It is recommended that the best practice for a foreign entrepreneur is to certainly be aware of all of these unique challenges and approach each of them with a *Minimum Viable Mindset (MVM)*.

A foreign entrepreneur with a minimum viable mindset (MVM) means that when you think of a business idea, always explore the shortest possible route to attain success or achieve that goal.

"It is better to work smarter than your competitor than harder than your competitor."

How you think

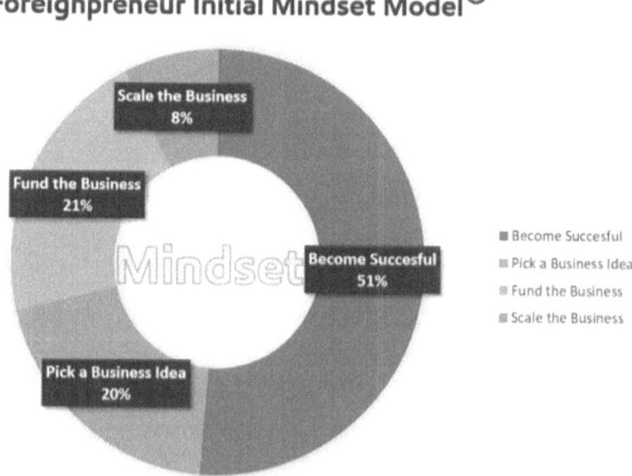

Fig 1.1 Initial mindset of a Foreign Entrepreneur

"Everyone has a plan until they are faced with reality."

At first glance, there is certainly nothing wrong with the initial mindset of a foreign entrepreneur in Figure 1.1 above, but on second glance, to think that most entrepreneurs, not just foreign entrepreneurs, are more preoccupied with becoming successful by any means that they lose track of the reality of delegating the capacity of their mind to other challenges that they have to solve, to be able to achieve their dream of building a successful business is almost surprising as a man who sets out on a journey only thinking of his final destination and forgetting to fuel his vehicle.

Who doesn't want to build a billion-dollar company? However, in reality, a foreign entrepreneur should learn to delegate the capacity of his or her mind to the real challenges such as picking a country, ideation, culture, building partnerships, relationship, family, funding, legal status, and regulations.

Hence, becoming successful should be the last thing to preoccupy the mind of a foreign entrepreneur. This is because if the entrepreneur can manage all the dependencies, such as picking a country, ideation, culture, building partnerships, relationship, family, funding, legal status, and regulations, the only reasonable goal would be the success.

Success is the goal that needs all the dependencies to work in favor of a foreign entrepreneur if he or she can succeed.

"Don't be too focused on the goal that you forget the struggles."

How you should think

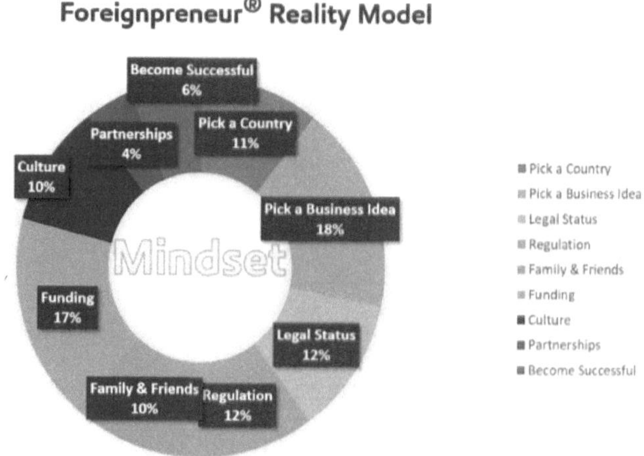

Fig 1.2 Foreignpreneur® Reality Model

The *Foreignpreneur® Reality Model* analyses the mind of a foreign entrepreneur from the point of reality rather than the fantasies of being the next Warren Buffet or Tim Cook in 100 days.

The reality of the hurdles that a foreign entrepreneur will have to scale through on a day to day basis is reflected in the —

Foreignpreneur® Reality Model by the recommended percentage of mind occupation based on my experiences and how I have delegated my mind. This is backed by a survey, which I sent to people, to disclose; *"What would be the first thing on their priority list when starting a business?"* I asked them to choose between picking a country, choosing a business idea, legal status, funding, partnership, regulations, culture, friends & family and becoming successful. eighty-four percent of the participants agree that their mind is preoccupied with success when starting a business. (See Appendix C)

The Foreignpreneur circle in Figure 1.2 will likely present the same challenges for most foreign entrepreneurs, but the percentage of mind occupation would vary in relation to events that occur in the life of that foreign entrepreneur on a person by person basis.

Rather than fixate your mind on being successful, delegate your mind to other things on your path to building a successful business. Unfortunately, in today's rapidly changing world of innovation where if you snooze you fail, entrepreneurs are meant to think like robots and are bombarded with hundreds, if not thousands of models from sales, development, marketing, success and startup models.

However, these models all have a missing piece: *The realities in the struggle of an entrepreneur's journey.*

An entrepreneur is a mom first before being an executive, a tenant before being a sales rep, a friend before being a marketing manager, needs a job before becoming a millionaire. So, you may ask, why then do most startup models provide entrepreneurs with acclaimed solutions on how to grow a business but neglect how the entrepreneur can overcome the hurdles and struggles that come with choosing the entrepreneurial path?

Little to no one talks about the failures of entrepreneurs. Models and stories are all flushed with how to become rich in 100 days. However, to become a successful foreign entrepreneur, you must understand those specific dependencies that can make or break you.

There is no secret to success, and there is nothing like a *Perfect Model.* Your life events, decisions, and actions are the most important in your journey, and no model or methodology can guarantee you success one-hundred percent; take that to the bank.

In the next chapters, we will discuss each of the dependencies in the *Foreignpreneur® Reality Model* based on personal experience(s). Each chapter is dedicated to one dependency and structured to give you a better understanding of what each of these challenges entails.

Chapter Two

How to Pick a Country?

Get Familiar with the Stats of Your New City

So much time, so little you know about your new landing pad for your entrepreneurship stardom when you choose a country that has less population, non-economic versatility, and stiff regulations.

This is a recipe for strangulation, not just for your business but your dream of being successful at what you do, unless success is a myth to you and only a word thrown around when you see an athlete driving a Ferrari.

Starting or expanding your business in a country with a large gross domestic product sounds impressive on the good books of basic economics; perhaps you should have coffee with the president of the international monetary fund (IMF), but on the other hand, this will not guarantee that an entrepreneur will thrive in a country, not to think of building a profitable enterprise.

A large percentage of foreign entrepreneurs choose countries based on decisions of friends, family, convenience or popularity of the destination. However, the more popular a city or a country is, the most likely that you may fail doing business in that city. That is because there is less chance of changing the status quo, and there's more to do.

Your uniqueness scale drops more than ever because there is a higher possibility that someone has already done what you are about to do or started a competing business. Most do not even bother with the economics of the country that they live in; you must know information such as the startup ecosystem, but this is so often overlooked.

If you intend to grow a business from a startup to a conglomerate, then you need a viable location, and one of the prerequisites is to consider answering the question: is there a demand for your product or service in the country you hope to incorporate your business? Do you have an in-depth knowledge of the market to understand the opportunities that your business can explore to grow into a profitable business?

You should consider researching first to see if there is.[2] If there's no demand, then there is no business. It's that simple. Review available research data to help you determine if your company's product and services are marketable overseas.[3]

A new business has a higher probability to grow from an idea to a startup company in emerging market, than in an already established market. Emerging markets are the sweet honey spot for the cooperate world to invest in. According to forbes.com, around 70% of the world's growth will come from emerging markets. These are markets whose economies are rapidly growing with room for improvement, a soft pad for an entrepreneurial dream and a sweet spot for a foreign entrepreneur.

However, in an already established market which has supportive business regulations, sound government policies and the ability of the foreign entrepreneur to wiggle his or her way through the nine dependencies, that startup business may grow into a billion-dollar multinational company.

For instance, an electricity distribution business may not thrive in Europe or America but could make you a billionaire in Africa. Nevertheless, doing business in Africa may have more stringent regulations and unfavorable government policies or even outdated technologies when compared to doing business in Europe or America. Again, the goal is to pick a country with favorable regulations, supportive government policies, good startup ecosystem, average or excellent standard of living and lots of business opportunities. This is better than a decision to start a business in a country that has the most significant gross domestic product, excellent standard of living but stiffer regulations, high cost of living, technologically advanced and a competitive market.

Of course, countries classified as emerging markets are no doubt attractive. However, a foreign entrepreneur must also be wary of bottlenecks in regulations in this type of market and always needs to:

"Settle, observe and take the opportunities that come."

An aspiring foreign entrepreneur will have a wide variety of places to choose from. In view of that, when looking to select a country to start your business, it is okay not to look for the next Silicon Valley, and it is also okay to understand that you will thrive in a country that has a viable startup ecosystem with all the opportunities of Silicon Valley than a country which has a large gross domestic product, no startup culture, bad economic policies, and nix business-friendly regulations.

Considering that you may have over 196 countries to choose from, selecting one can be mind-boggling. Therefore, applying these five steps may help to narrow it down.

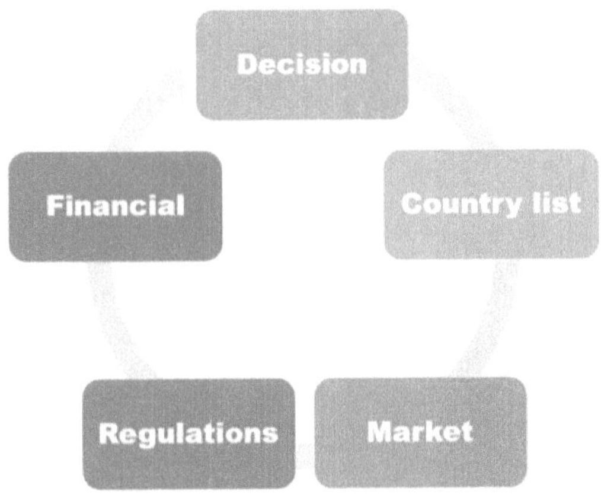

Fig 1.3 Foreignpreneur® five stages of picking a country

1. Analyze your decision

It can be tempting to skip a few steps when researching to select a country to do business, but this is one of the critical steps in the five stages. This is the stage of common sense.

Many foreign entrepreneurs default choice is the United States or the United Kingdom, without exploring other options. Jumping into quick decision regarding where to expand your —business or start a new one is clearly a no-go area but yet entrepreneurs are swayed by the fancy marketing campaigns of tourism departments of most countries. The reality is that every countries' commerce and tourism agency will present their country as the best destination to start a business or invest.

In 2016, I was approached by the United Kingdom trade and investment personnel to consider moving my mobile app company to the UK. The offer sounded very attractive with information such as listing on the London stock exchange (LSE) but on a second thought; I decided to give the decision a careful review.

First I wasn't sure what the future of *Brexit* withheld at the time, so I got back to the UK trade and investment and said *"Would you mind giving me a few contacts to investors, if I could secure an investment or have potential partnership on the table, I may consider the offer to move"*. My decision was solidified by the high cost of living in the UK compared to the financial risks that I was willing to take at that stage of the company.

The advantage of analytical thinking and consciousness is the first stage in deciding where or which country to choose. If I had taken up the offer from the UK trade and investment office without critically giving the opportunity a thought, that could have resulted in losing the chance to sit back in Budapest which was cheaper and favorable at the time with a growing economy and try to build my business to profitability before considering a move.

2. Make a list of countries

The second step is to make a list. When making this list, there are several factors to consider. This is not a list of the favorite countries on your bucket list, and you may be surprised to discover that your beloved country may not be the most viable location where you can start or expand a business.

Google Search may be your best friend at this point, and more in-depth research may help to narrow down your initial drive to write down almost every popular country you know. You may, however, consider the following:

2a. the Target Market

Are your target customers predominantly located in that country? Moreover, if yes, what are the statistics backing that assumption? You may also want to consider the type of technology your business needs to operate.

If you are going to start a solar business, find out how well solar technology has developed in the country you are about to choose. If you are considering a software company, try to figure out what business model other successful software companies in the same location have deployed to gain market share. Perhaps this may help you decide whether to go with a business to business (B2B) model, business to customer (B2C) or licensing, for example.

2b. Mobile Penetration

With the growth of the mobile industry and customers increasingly needing solutions to be delivered to their mobile devices, take a brief look at the mobile infrastructure available in the country that you intend to do business in.

However, this may depend on the type of business that you intend to build. Mobile penetration rate often leaves clues as to how technologically advance or open a target market is. Therefore, incorporating this as a criterion could be beneficial.

3. Competitive Landscape

When you draw a blueprint of the competitive landscape, you do not have to focus on the competitors you find on the first page of a Google search. It means looking at the entire ecosystem, including your competitors in other locations around the world. Even your closest competitor may decide to switch to your market.

When Facebook offered Snapchat billions to purchase, Snapchat turned it down, but Facebook went ahead to implement the famous Snapchat user stories which have since expanded into jobs, games, and marketplace; a hub for buying and selling.

Who would have thought that Facebook, a social networking app, would be a competitor to LinkedIn, or Amazon, a book selling online company, would become a competitor to Google?

Amazon has become a trillion-dollar technology giant, and one time, they were far from a leader in that market space. Therefore, it is essential to understand your wide scope competitors and those in your area so that you won't be taken by surprise.

The World Bank Group's ranking of economies will guide you on the ease of doing business in more than 180 countries. If there are competing products and services in your market of choice, you should be able to differentiate your offerings significantly enough to capture new customers?[4] Consider factors such as language, talent, economic stability, foreign exchange, and inflation.

3a. Immigration policy

When you are done with exploring the competitive landscape, studying the immigration policy of the country you've selected in Stage 1 could help prepare you on what to expect regarding residency.

Immigration is a global concern for many governments, but one thing they all agree is that having highly skilled individuals improves the economy and grows a robust human capital. Therefore, most governments have a more robust and supportive immigration law that makes it easy for a hardworking entrepreneur to integrate into their society to create jobs and pay tax.

Some of these include facilitating legal residential status and easy integration into the society for business owners who create jobs for the local communities.

Keep in mind that some countries have visas for highly skilled individuals which could be a good fit for a foreign entrepreneur while some don't. You can research countries which reward hardworking immigrants by enacting laws that protect their business.

Do not underestimate the importance of researching immigration policies when deciding to choose a country. If you do not have the correct documentation as a foreign founder or CEO, you can dream all you want, but when that immigration official comes knocking at your door, the civil rights groups or a lawyer can do little to save your business.

Consider the different types of legal documentation required in the country you have chosen in Stage 1 before proceeding to Stage 2, as this will enable you to focus on building your business rather than having to deal with all the hassles of legal documentation while also dealing with other dependencies.

3b. Taxation

Tax is an obligation that has to be met under any circumstance, and not meeting this obligation may not only result in the failure of your business but could land you in jail. Educating yourself on taxation issues can help save you money and a possible brush with the law as you wiggle your way through the early stages of your business.

When registering your business, the country you choose vis-à-vis taxation matters. A significant percentage of foreign entrepreneurs face critical tax issues. Often, they could end up with double taxation for countries that have cooperative international tax laws with their home country.

This means that as foreign founder of a startup company, regardless of the country that you've decided to start a business, you will be taxed by your country of origin and residence, and provided you remain a citizen of the latter, you may end up being taxed by two governments.

To avoid double taxation, be sure to read the international tax co-operation between your native country and the country you do business.

By paying attention to some of these issues, foreign entrepreneurs can position themselves to take advantage of some tax benefits and avoid taxation problems.

Consider taxation as an investment in your business that you have to pay dividends for. Therefore, no matter how you view tax, it merely means that the government is like a shareholder in your business with no voting rights, and you have to pay dividends. Which means:

"Give to Cesar what belongs to Cesar." — Mark 12:17

You can only find ways to limit the amount of taxation for your business by starting your company in a country that has a favorable tax policy. However, avoiding tax is tantamount to ruining your life and not just being a failed entrepreneur.

There are countries with better tax incentives than others. Think about it this way. If you can get a favorable taxation policy such as — tax relief in *"Country X" than in "Country Z," why would you choose Country Z" over Country X"?* This is where common sense is applied.

For example, the United States has the fourth highest statutory corporate income tax rate in the world, levying a 38.91 percent tax on corporate earnings. The only jurisdictions with a higher statutory rate are the United Arab Emirates, Comoros, and Puerto Rico. Europe has the lowest regional average rate, at 18.35 percent (25.58 percent when weighted by GDP). Conversely, Africa and South America tie for the highest regional average statutory rate at 28.73 percent (28.2 percent weighted by GDP for Africa, 32.98 percent weighted by GDP for South America).

In general, large industrialized nations tend to have higher statutory corporate income tax rates than developing countries. [5]

What that means is, you have to think of developing economies and emerging markets over large industrialized nations. Keep in mind; this is not a smooth pass to success as other factors can affect your business in developing countries beyond taxation.

If you wish to register your business in a country that has a tax rate of thirty-five percent, then you should probably think about an alternative country with a lower tax rate.

If you are offering a service or a product, the location of your servers can also affect your taxation and not just on paper. This could also affect the availability of your service in certain countries, as the laws of that location sometimes govern your server location; for example, having a server in the USA means U.S. laws may apply including U.S. export laws and may also limit availability in the case of a mobile app business when you select your applicable stores.

4. Financials

4a. Loans

Starting a business is easy; sustaining the business is hard. Those few savings will only get you a few miles ahead in your journey to create a sustainable business.

Consider lack of finance and entrepreneurship as a modern car whose driver is running on an empty fuel tank. The driver may have the driving experience required, which, in this scenario, is entrepreneurial experience but without fuel (capital) to drive the car to the driver's destination, the driver is unable to complete the journey. This is what having limited — or no access to a loan, grants or financial stability to start and run a business looks like.

"In 1995, Elon Musk and his brother Kimbal founded Zip2 with twenty-eight thousand dollars out of their father's bank account. Four years later, it was acquired by Compaq for three hundred and seven million dollars, with Elon making twenty-two million dollars. A little under a month later, he put ten million dollars of that into co-founding X.com, which he envisioned to be the future of online banking. A year after, it merged with Confinity to create PayPal."[6]

"In June 2002, Elon Musk founded SpaceX using some of the twelve million dollars he had left over from Zip2. Then in October, PayPal was acquired for one and half billion and being the company's largest shareholder, Elon made hundred and sixty-five million. With this large sum of money, Elon later allocated about ninety million dollars to SpaceX, which could have gone to waste had he not taken a crucial investment from Draper Fisher Jurveston in 2008."[7]

"In 2006, Elon became a significant investor who jumpstarted his cousin's company Solar City, of which he is currently chairman. From 2003-2009, he had spent over seventy million dollars of his own money to ensure the longevity of —Tesla Motors. For a time, he was chairman, lead investor, and head designer but wasn't CEO until 2008 when the company nearly spiraled into bankruptcy after missing out on a hundred-million-dollar investment. These companies, each of which had their fair share of financial crises, is now worth billions of dollars today."[8]

"Elon would go on to say in interviews that he ran into debt and lived in rented apartments after taking up new adventures to set up some of his most prominent companies that we now know today as Tesla, SpaceX, and the Boring Company".

You would have thought, one-hundred and sixty-five-million-dollar sure sound like a cool ton of money, but Elon ran out of financial fuel regardless of his vast experience from PayPal. The glaring reality for a foreign entrepreneur is, of course, the undeniable factor that you must get your hands on financial support. There is literarily no publicly traded company without investors, and these are the big wigs in the various industries; they all have and need investments to compete unless you are building a business for just you and your family.

Examine your access to loans, grants and investment opportunities for your business when making a list of countries in Stage 2. Make sure to research investment opportunities, loan, and the grants available in the country you've chosen.

Think of venture capitalists, angel investors, contemplate a thorough research of the financial landscape of the country and the fabric that makes up the financial ecosystem, including grants by the government of that country to support equal access to funding to finance local and international business.

If you decide to fund your business through a bank loan, make sure to seek financial and legal advice for which type of loan you should be applying. For example, going for a — personal loan could be tricky if you have not yet validated your market and your products because you may still run into roadblocks that may leave you with not only a failed business but a debt to pay off.

4c. Payment

Ask your potential customers what their preferred method of payment is. Chances are they already have experience with international transactions through e-payment. It is a critical step to learn how to collect payment on overseas sales and transactions. This is the single most vital, yet insanely overlooked detail.[9]

Payments are now evolving at a rapid pace with new providers, new platforms, and new payment tools launching on a near-daily basis.[10] You may need to consider if your option would be mobile payment, online payment, bank transfer or even cash.

As a foreign entrepreneur, registering and setting up a bank account(s) could be a daunting task, one where you may end up wishing you had a piggy bank in your wardrobe to save you the drama; however, one problem with a piggy bank is its limited capacity. On a more serious note, banking and financial transactions for a foreign entrepreneur require you to scrutinize your options.

The paperwork for opening an account and setting up a financial structure for your business may depend on the country you have chosen. Some countries still have laws that limit the ability of a foreigner with certain legal status to open a bank account, and at the same time, study the demographics of your target market to determine which payment options to incorporate in your business.

I remember going to some European banks where I would often get responses such as "Unfortunately we do not open an account for people from your country." I call this —systematic discrimination, and while this might sound weird, this is the reality that some foreign entrepreneurs face.

In 2016, I had just finished developing version 5.0 of my Study in Europe mobile app, and even though the interface was sleek and easy to use, conversion was a nightmare. Users were unable to pay, and the majority of my users at the time were from Africa as most media outlets who reviewed my app at the time were in Nigeria.

I tried integrating PayPal which is one of the leading payment processing systems, but PayPal had just limited its services in Nigeria to few features that would make it difficult for customers in Nigeria to transact through its platform. I had to come up with an alternative payment method, and I found PayStack. The PayStack Company were processing over a billion naira at the time with a simple, sleek interface which would enable the verse percentage of my mobile app users in Nigeria to make payments through the app, and my other target market, which was made up of India and the United States could make their payments through PayPal.

As the importance of payment became glaring, I knew technology was the only viable option for a foreign entrepreneur to limit the impact of a payment bottleneck for international business, so I considered countries with advanced payment technologies such as e-payment systems.

An e-payment system is a way of making transactions or paying for goods and services through an electronic medium without the use of checks or cash. It's also called an automated payment system or an online payment system.[11]

5. Concluding your final selection

After going through the five stages of picking a country, you may still be drawn to selecting the country of your childhood dreams or recommendation from a friend. However, in business and to succeed in life, you will need to make the hard decision and painstakingly back those decisions. Becoming a business founder or an executive is hard, and building one as a foreigner is even harder.

Keep in mind that choosing a location goes beyond taxation. Some customers may prefer to purchase a *Made in USA product* over *Made in China product or Made in China product* over *Made in USA*, so before you put together your beautifully constructed "About us page" on your company website, think about where you want to incorporate your business and which information is an advantage to your credibility.

Information such as incorporation date, location, and telephone number are subtle information that can sway a customer. However, you can decide which way you swing them with that information.

When choosing a country, think of the country from the lens of a hustler, a country that you can dream, where you can get support from an already established business ecosystem with favorable economic policies and regulations, with room for emerging technologies and don't forget to hustle, hustle, and hustle.

"Every successful entrepreneur was once a hustler."

Chapter Three

Choosing a Business

Find the honey spot of your business model

*S*tarting and running a business in a new city will require you to redefine your business model to match the demographics and audience. As much as you analyze the technical background, read books on startup models, seek funding and grow your workforce, you also need to prioritize and consider the various cultural differences that you need to incorporate into your marketing model; finding and defining that model isn't an easy walk down an escalator.

When creating a product or service in a new society, a foreign entrepreneur would need to deeply consider what's available in the new society over what he or she may have regarded as the super model– there is nothing like a "super model."

Think of this scenario as a simple example of buying a new iPhone which has new functionalities. However, you have no clue how each of these new functionalities works and why —the heck would you even need those functionalities?

Obviously, it would help if you had time to understand the new device which does not necessarily mean that you are not smart enough to operate an iPhone. It simply means that:

"When you are in Rome behave like Romans,[if you know what I mean?]"—Saint Ambrose

Choosing a business to start in new society is a formidable challenge. There are competitively priced alternatives to almost every service or product, and emerging technologies, policy prerogative and societal choices can all affect your choice of business.

Some countries may prefer to purchase cheaper products, perhaps due to their societal norm of not attaching value to luxury, while on the other hand, some countries may consider luxury items as a means of social status.

For example, in Nigeria, wealth and connections are seen as high social status, so perhaps buying a Mercedes Benz whose market value is two hundred thousand euros may be applauded in Nigeria. Compare this to Hungary where buying the same Mercedes Benz for two hundred thousand may be considered less important.

Overpricing your product could be an example of not doing proper research on the cultural indexes. Assuming that your new society would pay more for a service or product that costs less in a society that you are already accustomed, and if you were wrong, the balance sheets will come crashing down, and trust me sacking your most talented accountant won't save your business.

Hence, society pressure, culture and the court of public opinion leave a vital clue for a foreign entrepreneur when creating a new business model in a new society.

Most entrepreneurs focus hard on building an innovative product but forget that an elegant solution doesn't automatically translate into a successful business. Businesses require an equally elegant business model with the right price, messaging and delivery channel to the right target customers to keep the dream alive and growing.[12]

Therefore, when creating a business model or advertising to members of a different culture, always research the target market prior to beginning the campaign. Levels of conservatism, gender views and ideologies can vary significantly between cultures. Presenting a campaign that is not in line with specific cultural norms can insult the target audience and greatly hinder the campaign. Being aware of cultural norms can also help your company narrow down the target audience. For instance, in Japan and Austria, men are usually in control of the decision-making, but women make the majority of purchasing decisions in Sweden.[13]

When I was developing the subscription model for my mobile app travel company, I considered the need that international students seeking to study abroad usually pay higher consultancy fees to university agents to secure them university admission abroad. These fees run into thousands of euros, in excess of one- two thousand euros, and yet they can be denied entry for simple reasons such as submitting invalid documents.

So, when I was coming up with a service charge in my model, I considered that these international students would be delighted to pay somewhere between four hundred to six hundred euros for a similar service but this time using my mobile application service. My service would connect students directly to universities and offer travel services such as airport taxi, accommodation, flight, travel insurance, and visa application as add-on services without the need to apply through the university or travel agents.

Brilliant? Right! Yeah, that's what I thought at the first instance while creating my pricing plan.

Oh boy! I was dead wrong. I discovered that specific locations where my app was downloaded considered the cost relatively cheap while some thought it was too high, even though they could get the same service from a third party university agent for four times the price of using a mobile app in minutes.

I discovered that if your product or service is too expensive for the market, then there is a higher risk that you won't succeed, and when your prices are too low, this may also leave you exposed and running on an empty balance sheet. So, I needed to figure out something real quick. Otherwise, I would be in deep water with the cost of servers which skyrockets each time a user downloads the mobile app.

So, I did what I usually do best, I turned on my Xbox video game console and played some video games, my favorite position when things are not going right. I love to play video games; they stimulate my brain and gets me thinking.

FIFA is my favorite game, and so I selected my team and was about to kick off the game, an idea came to mind; *"Since people could buy the FIFA game at different prices across various regions or countries"* then perhaps what I need to solve my mobile app pricing problem is to have different prices by —region or country, while incorporating the cultural differences into that price.

I immediately connected the local market distribution dots to my pricing plan, and came up with a unified pricing plan of somewhere between five dollars and nine dollars, making sure to check my currency converter to get the local prices of each and every store where my mobile application would be sold. It turned out, it gave me a clearer picture of how much each market would be willing to pay. I supported my plan with research on the various business models that other mobile app companies were using to come up with their pricing plan in those specific markets.

This meant that I had to switch my business model to suit each market and to recognize that choosing a business is interconnected to its business model. If I could not sell out a unit of my app, then there is no business, zero! It's as simple as that. On the other hand, success with the business meant developing the right model and choosing the right business to apply that model.

One important reason to consider when developing a business model before choosing a business is that you can apply your business model to other businesses, regardless of which industry or sector. For example, the third party middleman business model can be found in most industries today, starting with Insurance companies.

Today, we've got the likes of Uber and AirBnB doing the middle man or the third party model using technology. Let's be clear; the Uber and AirBnB model are the same. For Uber, they provide drivers a platform to enlist their profiles and, in turn, these drivers drive for Uber while Uber connect them to customers looking for a ride.

For AirBnB, on the other hand, they provide an online platform for homeowners to list their homes for short stays and, in turn, AirBnB connects them to customers looking for an apartment for short stay rent.

"Similar model, different business."

Your business model or strategy is the first step in choosing a business and to do that as a foreign entrepreneur; you would need to consider other dependencies that I have listed in the nine dependencies of the *Foreignpreneur® Reality Model.* For example, culture, language, and regulation is an integral part of your choosing a business process.

An entrepreneur needs to consider developing a business model, as his or her first step in choosing a business by conducting a thorough research on how the success of that business model is feasible in the country that the entrepreneur wishes to do business. This is because a business model that works perfectly in China may not work well in the United States, even though they may have the same model. Take culture for example:

When I decided to expand my drink distribution business in Nigeria by adding a few competitive products. I considered an energy drink, known as *"Hell."* The product was perfect for the market, the packaging was right, the taste, the history, and you name it. Moreover, selling the product to Africa's largest population who loved to live life to the fullest didn't seem like a hard knock to crack either, but one thing stood in the way. Guess what? *Religion!*

Nigeria has thousands of registered churches where pastors are equated to God and almost as important as the president. The name *"Hell"* for the majority of Christians in Nigeria could be a significant deterrent to purchasing the product.

In inference, this was enough to make me have a rethink. Although I considered re-labeling to ***"Hello,"*** but that would take away the strength of the marketing of the parent brand. That meant a new, unknown brand, and promoting a new brand doesn't come cheap. Again, culture and religion played a role in my decision to pass that business opportunity. Think about it this way:

"A new society = A new target audience."

So, to address some of my challenges of picking a business model, I came up with a list of dos and don't which I call the Foreignpreneur® 4 rules of choosing a business and model.

Foreignpreneur® Four Rules of Choosing a Business Model

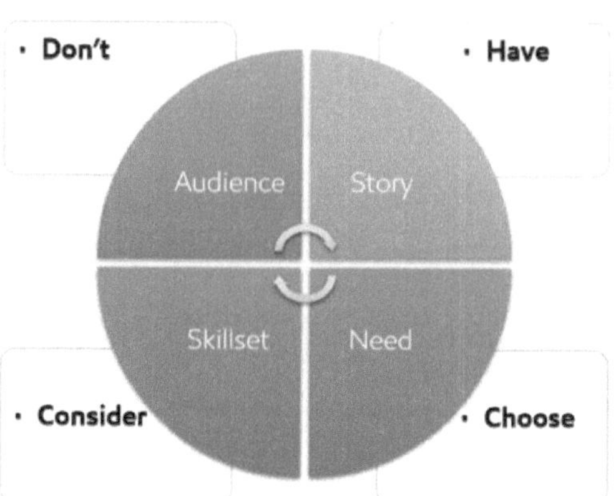

1. Do not create a business that only targets your native audience

There is likely the slightest probability that you will not find someone from the same country as you in your new society on a networking event; it is a rare phenomenon when compared to connecting with new people in your new society for the same type of event. In retrospect, there is a higher probability on the other end of the scale that you will connect with more people from different cultures and community in a foreign country than in your native country, and you will also see already existing communities of people from the same country as you, which —you are naturally drawn to.

Many aspiring foreign entrepreneurs create small scale businesses targeting their native communities living abroad. However, this limits the business reach to a small audience. As a foreign entrepreneur, you should strive to tap into the curiosity of your new society, expand your market and create a business that targets the larger population of your new audience. For example, if you are a British citizen living in South Africa, create a business that targets both British citizens living in South Africa and South Africans residing in South Africa. Do not limit your audience to only British citizens living in South Africa and thereby, cutting off the larger end of the pie which is South Africans living in South Africa.

"An entrepreneur loses the wow effect when he or she focuses on a market that already knows the product."

A Chinese citizen would catch the wow effect tasting the local cuisines of Tanzania than eating the local Chinese cuisine which he or she is already used to, no matter how well-prepared the dish is served.

2. Have a story behind your brand

Have a story and turn your story to profit. People need a hero, someone to look up to, and people want to know that someone is experiencing or has experienced the same challenges as them. When you find it, connect it to your business.

Entrepreneurs are made by the people who purchase their products, and the personality or beliefs of their founders are shaping public opinion. Today, individuals have metamorphosed through social media platforms like Instagram and Twitter into brands.

Consider the case study of how celebrities and influencers build up follower-ship on social media as this can help you understand why brands pay a tremendous amount of money to have access to fans of branded individuals with a significant amount of followers; you can build follower-ship with your story, make it worth it!

"It is better to stay close to your customers than your investors. No entrepreneur is self-made."

One of the reasons that you need to sell your story is that people are more likely to buy the music of a homeless man who found his way to the colored lights of the O2 arena, a perfect —rag to riches story, than a rich kid who made it in the same industry through hard work. This is because they can relate to the homeless man and will always perceive the rich to own what they could have owned.

If you can't find the sweet honey spot of your business, then create one through the connection of your story to your business model.

3. Choose a business that solves a problem over what you are passionate about

Wait a minute? What did I suggest, forget *Passion*? Everyone says you should do what you are passionate about, why shouldn't you? Well, capital, experience, and skillset can get an entrepreneur from point A to point B, but passion will keep you going regardless of the ups and downs along your journey. However, this does not mean that every hobby should be a business.

Just because you are passionate about flying kites doesn't mean you will make a living or build a business flying a kite. If people do not need a person who flies kites, your passion for flying kites will not get you anywhere other than debts and frustration.

Every business started to solve a problem. Google, Apple, Tesla all solve problems, and I bet that everyone in the boardroom of Tesla is not passionate about self-driving cars or green energy. The same applies to every Google investor. I am sure you would agree with me that not every one of them knows Jack about technology; they may not even be able to turn on an Apple air pod for their kids, but they all have one thing in common. They are successful because their product or service is solving a problem.

Don't crucify me yet; you need passion alright, but that should not be the only driving factor when choosing a business. Think of a problem that requires a solution and make sure your business is providing that solution before being passionate about it.

I hardly comment on social media platforms such as YouTube, Facebook, and Twitter, not because I dislike them, but I believe there is an element of neglect to the data behind the comments on these platforms, and we all understand how they are shaping our society. No one's asked what's the age, gender, cultural view behind the account of social media users expressing their opinion through millions of likes, comments and shares.

I watched my little niece comment on a feminist video on YouTube by typing, "All men are wicked." Of course, I knew she was around ten years old at the time, and she has no clue what feminism is about, but her opinion counted amongst the metrics of number of comments, likes and views that even mainstream media such as CNN, Fox news would air on their platform as hashtags and news of the day. We need to start questioning social media on who is commenting, liking and sharing these opinions.

However, that is irrelevant to the context of the topic that this book is trying to address. I finally commented on a YouTube channel but this time on a video of a young Nigerian girl who was an entrepreneur and had just finished her studies in Europe and moved back to Nigeria. In her twelve minutes video, she complained bitterly about not being successful after moving back to Nigeria. She narrated how frustrated she was about not starting her clothing brand, which she is passionate about. However, something else caught my attention, which made me leave a comment.

She said *"Everything is expensive in Nigeria. I ate a plate of food for five thousand naira."* Mind you, five thousand Nigerian naira, is roughly about twenty euros for a plate of food to which I replied:

"If you bought a plate of food for five thousand naira, that right there is the opportunity that you just missed. I think that opening a food chain or restaurant to compete with the excessive cost of a plate of food for five thousand naira could undoubtedly make you much money. Get your price between one thousand five hundred to two thousand five hundred naira and still be able to make the interior of your restaurant look nice. Find a carpenter, look up a picture on Pinterest for some

crazy design ideas and leave the rest to a Nigerian local carpenter. Trust me; he will give you the Nigerian version of [Mark Zuckerberg's] wardrobe.

Imagine having Kentucky Fried Chicken-styled menus for Nigerian local dishes such as Akara (Nigerian fries), Bread, and Cola projected on the screens just like you see in sweet sensation and McDonald's. All those office managers can come in and eat hot Akara as snacks on their way home or during lunch.

Secondly, the Nigerian economy is not as favorable as it was a few years back; you should look at businesses in essential commodities, not by passion. Passion is overhyped. What you need is to provide goods or services that solve a problem. A perfect example of a failed plan would be opening a car [dealership] or real estate business [When the economy is shrinking]. The reason why this would not work is that the purchasing power in Nigeria is currently down, and people would instead buy food, recharge cards, pay for tuition than— buy a car or rent an expensive apartment.

My comment at the time was addressing two factors: business needs over passion and the ability for the foreign entrepreneur to study the new business climate and imbibe the cultural differences into her marketing strategy. However, her situation was choosing passion over the current realities of the country she has just moved to, in this case, Nigeria.

She was still stuck with the culture and way of doing business from the country where she moved from in Budapest, Hungary. She needed to face reality, redefine her model and choose the right business that works in the country she now lives in — Nigeria.

4. Consider your skill set

Let me make this one a little easier. Let's analyze a scenario where you are competent at computer repairs. You have spent ten years working for a multinational computer manufacturing company, and you've decided to start a computer repair business. You've got all the experience and skill set needed from the IT industry, so you are all set and good to go.

Let's roll it back again and analyze a different scenario. This time, let's assume that you have no experience in web development, but you would like to start a web development training school, and you have no clue where to start. What you need and who to hire. Can you teach programming? Do you know how to select the right tutor(s) for your computer training school? When starting a business, going into unfamiliar territory with no skill set will limit your innovation and slow you down.

Have you ever thought about what Michael Faraday, the inventor of electric motor, would achieve without knowledge of Physics? In the current world of business, you either innovate or you fail. Customers barely spend less than a minute considering a new product or service because there's always an alternative for almost every product.

The question you should ask yourself as an entrepreneur is; how long would it take me to build company X instead of company Y? If the amount of time, energy and skill set needed to build company X is less than company Y, start with company X.

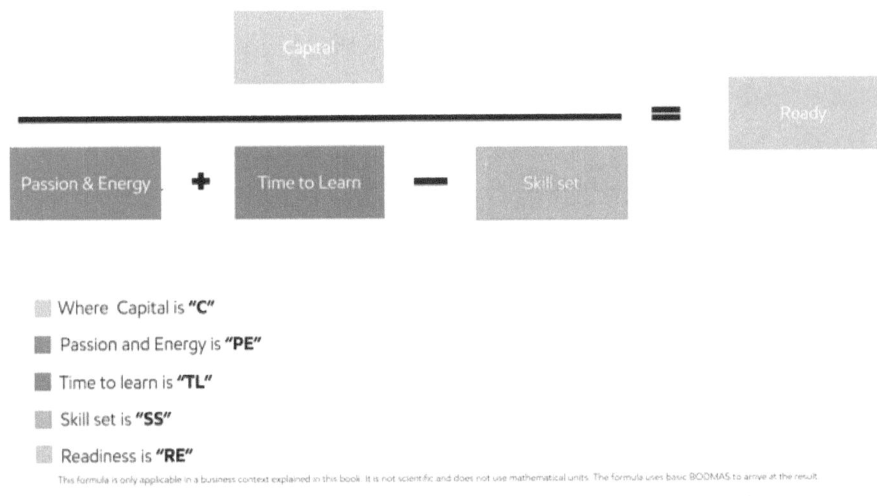

Fig 1.3 Foreignpreneur® Comparison Formula

Here's an example using the formula:

Scenario One:

Aytan is an Azerbaijani, who would like to start a Turkish Kebab business in Budapest, Hungary. Aytan had just arrived Budapest six months ago. At the initial stage, Aytan needs five skill set as pre-requirements to start her Kebab business. She will need language, communication, sales, cooking, and marketing skills.

Aytan has previous cooking experience working in a local restaurant in Azerbaijan and has an excellent cooking skill, —which means Aytan has met one out of five skill requirements for her Kebab business.

Aytan will need a period of two years to learn the language, communication, sales, and marketing skills. On a scale of one to hundred percent, Aytan feels she has a passion and energy of fifty percent and has access to funding of ten thousand euros.

Scenario Two:

Michael, a US national, has just arrived in Germany and would like to start an online store. At the initial stage, Michael needs five skills as

pre-requirements to start his online store. He will need language skills, communication skills, web development skills, sales skills and marketing skills.

Michael has visited Germany a couple of times in the past and understands German at proficiency level because Michael's family is half German, half American, which means he already has the language skill set. Therefore, Michael is at one out of five skill required for his online store.

Since Michael understands the culture and language, he would need one year to learn web development, before he can start his online store business. On a scale of one to hundred percent, — Michael feels he has a passion and energy of 50 percent and has access to funding of ten thousand euros.

Let's calculate using the Foreignpreneur® comparison formula, between Michael and Aytan who is ready? To find out first, let's quantify and unitize their abilities and capabilities.

In calculating the readiness of Michael and Aytan, there are higher chances that Michael could succeed in building a successful online store in Germany than Aytan. However, Michael's success would also be contingent on navigating the other dependencies listed in the *Foreignpreneur® Reality Model* in Chapter Two.

When you compare the situation for the two foreign entrepreneurs, you discover that the readiness value of Michael is higher than that of Aytan, which means that Michael has a —good chance of hitting the ground running. Aytan may incur the cost of delays if she starts her Kebab business with incompetent skills or lacking pre-requisite skills.

This formula can also be applied when a Foreign entrepreneur is at a crossroad of choosing between two business ideas to scale. I have added an exercise at the end of this book (See worksheet in Appendix) to calculate your unique situation.

Fig 1.4 Foreignpreneur® Readiness Model

The Foreignpreneur readiness model looks to compare the time needed for an entrepreneur to build a business from an idea to the point of implementation in relation to having the pre-requisite skillset and capital to actualize the business.

If you need proper sales skill to start your conference marketing company, and you've only acquired fifty percent of the sales skill required, but you have a time constraint to go into the market, then consider starting an alternative business in which you have the required hundred percent skill set. At least, you can then hit the ground running from an idea to the implementation stage.

This will enable you to validate your market, have a timely working prototype, and limit any potential cost of delay caused by not having the pre-requisite skill set. You could also avoid giving room to other potential competitors to enter the market before you. Acquiring a new skill set would require your time, money and energy, which you could instead use to grow your idea from conceptualization to implementation.

You may still be able to fund your alternative company in the future by hiring a skilled workforce. However, hiring employees at the beginning may swell the capital you require to start your business, and you don't want to take that path when you are yet to validate your market.

Finally, there are a couple of businesses you can do as a foreign entrepreneur. I have put together a couple of them from my list of favorites. Yours may well be different, but it won't hurt — to share:

1. Food Business:

One of the easy-to-do businesses as a foreign entrepreneur is a restaurant chain business.

Nonetheless, you have to start small while thinking big. Be that as it may, when building this type of business, there is a cultural and curiosity aspect to having your country's local dish sold to a broad audience in your new society. A United States citizen would love to taste the local Nigerian "Jollof Rice" dish than the traditional United States burger, simply because we are wired to be curious about uncertainty, and this opens an opportunity for you to explore this curiosity while making money.

2. Importation and Exportation:

When you arrive in a new country, there is always one or more necessities missing. For example, some countries have large deposits of crude oil, while some have large deposits of gold. Some are rich in agriculture with fertile soil while some need to survive through the importation of agricultural products.

Should you start by exporting or importing these necessities? The answer is yes, and this gap can be explored easily as a foreign entrepreneur if your native country has products or services needed in your new society. You can use your local knowledge to your advantage by exporting to your new society and make your sales at a higher price. Alternatively, you can consider selling through an intermediary (trading company) which could buy your product locally and re-sell to its distribution base of customers in a foreign country.

3. Technological gaps in society:

Mostly influenced by your choice of country, take, for example, the mobile penetration rate in Nigeria is much higher than in Haiti, and a high percentage of Nigerians still top-up their mobile phones through printed recharge cards. Compare this to Hungary where mobile phone top-up is done through POS machines.

As a foreign entrepreneur, spotting technology gaps can help you find the right idea to build a business. If your country of origin has a self-driving car culture, and your new society does not then consider bringing that technology with you and making a business from it. That's the fastest way to turn a technology gap into a business.

4. Language Consultancy:

If your language is the hardest language in the world, then someone somewhere in the world may want to learn that language for a fee. Speak to a man in a language he understands[14], and you most certainly have won the heart.

Language is essential to most businesses that want to expand to new markets, especially in the area of customer service and personal development. For example, if you are a Norwegian living in the Philippines, then consider starting a language school that teaches the Norwegian language to Filipinos and international communities living in the Philippines.

5. Fashion:

How many times did you try or felt an urge to wear the traditional attire of a foreign culture? The fashion industry is a vast multi-billion-dollar pool that you can —tap into by selling clothes made from the fabrics of your country of origin; this business has a reach beyond the country you live and is categorized as an essential commodity. Unless we return to the "Stone Age", humans will always need clothes to wear, and you can be in the business of providing those clothes with a touch of tradition from your country while making money.

6. Beauty Saloon or Hair Saloon:

If your country has a unique hair style that your country of residence or the international community would be curious about, then you can offer services in this space and build a business from it. Although this type of business has a limited target audience, you can still invest or start your own business in this space.

7. Real Estate:

Housing deficit is a global problem in almost every country in the world, and the growing demand will continue to as long as the population boom is not addressed. I have considered adding this to the list simply because to build a real estate business; you need to know three basic principles: cost, location, and the economy of the country where you are buying, building or selling.

According to Real Capital Analytics (RCA), global volumes for completed sales of commercial properties totalled eight hundred and seventy-three billion dollars, matching the total registered in 2016. A six percent rise in the Asia Pacific and an eight percent increase in Europe offset a decline in the US, the world's largest commercial real estate investment market. Real estate continues to attract capital, demonstrating its appeal over other asset classes in an otherwise uncertain investment world that is starting to betray signs of nervousness over inflation and rising interest rates.[15]

Subsequently, the best business for a foreign entrepreneur is one which connects home and abroad. Combining the two cultures gives the entrepreneur the best of both worlds, and a foreign entrepreneur should strive to find this type of business idea.

Chapter Four

Regulations

Don't get locked up; your credit score is key

Any new business or technology is directly affected by the laws, regulations, and policies of a government. If a government feels that a technology threatens their control or has an uncertain outcome, they will find ways to regulate that technology, so keep this in mind when building your next Space X. Also keep in mind to stay away from politics as much as you can and only get involved if it directly affects your business. Do not underestimate the power of government and the laws that they enact.

It is vital to get legal help in both your new city and your native country to keep you updated with regulations and the laws to guide you through the uncertainties of creating a new business abroad.

Some countries have different regulations on a city by city basis, and a foreign entrepreneur must be aware of the laws and regulation of the city they live in as well as the country. In most cases, federal and state laws may apply.

When I first received an auto insurance bill of three hundred euros in the mailbox in November of 2017, the first thought that came to my mind was *"the insurance company had better have a valid explanation.*

Why I need to pay as high as one month's salary for most average workers?" I was confident in my mind that I did not owe the insurance company, and neither did I see any reason why I got a letter with a three hundred euro fine. I could book a flight to Paris and still keep some change with that kind of money.

So I jumped into my *Massimo Dutti* blue checked jeans and a *Polo Ralph Lauren* T-shirt, all dressed up to demand my rights. When I stepped into the auto insurance office, I was sure that nowhere in my contract did it say I had to renew automatically if it expired.

However, one question hung in the balance. **"When I signed in the first instance, did I read the auto insurance terms and conditions?"** Moreover, even if I wanted to read the terms and conditions, what language were they written in? Well, they were written in Hungarian, and I didn't understand a word of it. — Nada!

Many of us just glance through the terms and conditions and don't really care what we accept or sign on to, simply because we don't have the time or because there's the slightest chance that you will have issues from accepting the terms. However, each time you accept the terms and condition without reading it, you risk leaving yourself exposed to a potential lawsuit.

It turned out I was supposed to renew my insurance more than six months ago, and I didn't, so I had already accumulated fines from the government and the insurance company.

Now if I had read the contract, I may have saved myself a three-hundred-euro bill that I could have invested in my business. Nonetheless, I ended up paying the fine, and luckily, this did not affect my credit score. I soon found out, however, that in getting new auto insurance, the insurance companies would have to reference my history of overdue fines which ultimately meant my insurance cost would shoot up.

As simple as it seemed, this could have easily gotten me in front of a judge and dent my reputation or credit score, and as a foreign entrepreneur with a dream of building a business, you don't want to be in that position.

When you break the law or live in the naivety of the law, you expose yourself to the possibility of having problems with the law. And if this leads to court appearances, fines or even jail time, best believe it will be an uphill task to turn around your fortune, because most employers of labour and potential business partners do background checks.

Every foreign entrepreneur must be aware of legal obligations, terms, and conditions, whether written in your native language or the language of the country you live and do business. A lack of awareness could not only land you in a series of fines but also bring down your credit score.

There are many situations where foreigners have built up businesses, but due to minor offenses like speeding tickets, unpaid fine, unreported change of residential address has led to the revocation of their legal status. It may seem like minor offenses, but no offense is minor when viewed from the goggles of a foreigner. Be on your best behavior and follow the regulations.

Regulations can destroy a startup business without even meaning to. In many countries, the number of steps required to incorporate a new company is staggering: business license, employment reporting, tax collection, mandatory training, and more. Apart from the cost of these regulations, there is also the psychological burden of learning what they all mean and worrying that you may have missed one of them and will be found liable, which can ruin your business and put you back right where you started.

For a local or citizen of a country, there is a higher possibility that he or she is already aware of some of these regulations, but a foreign entrepreneur has little or no knowledge and so much ground to cover. You could always seek legal advice, but this won't come cheap, and all these could add up to the capital of the business. Nonetheless, if your situation is different and somehow, you have access to lots of money, you may as well hire a legal team to take care of everything related to the business regulations.

"You are never invincible. You can be controlled, no matter how smart you are, there is always someone better."

Therefore, do not bother outsmarting the law but find ways within the constitution to thrive.

Ensure that you have legal residency status in your new city. Your residency increases your chance of eligibility for loans, mortgages, grants and helps cut down regulations; every country has a different set of rules applicable to citizens and foreigners, and you should put yourself in a position of strength.

In 2013, when I began my master's degree in communications and media studies, I briefly thought about the possibility of studying with a scholarship, but I never believed I needed one. Besides, anything free is a trade by barter. However, I quickly realized how expensive it was to pay over three thousand, five hundred euros per semester for a course that is over fifty percent cheaper for citizens. This meant that the regulations for some international students are different from those of locals or citizens.

Also, you may ask, are the lectures or curriculum different? The answer is No. Students were paying cheaper tuition but studying in the same class and acquiring the same knowledge as me simply because they had different resident status.

The only grant or benefit you can get as a student is scholarships, discounted cinema tickets, metro tickets and lots of party tickets, and I'm pretty sure you weren't considering a party ticket enough grant for your world-changing business idea. Some may argue that a scholarship gives you breathing space to gain more knowledge and strategies for your business, but it doesn't pay your bills and neither would it take care of your servers or your payroll.

Legal residency is like your steering; it may determine the direction where you can build partnerships and where you can try out new possibilities. The chart below explains the common types of legal residency status that a foreign entrepreneur can obtain in a new society and the legal rights, access to loans and travel flexibility.

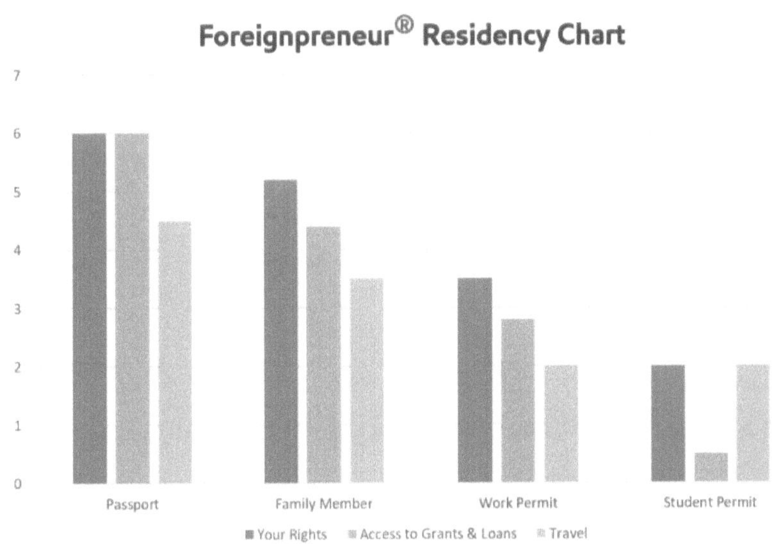

Fig 1.5 Foreignpreneur® Residency Chart

It is essential not to underestimate the importance of certain categories of legal residency status.

For example, a foreign entrepreneur who has a temporary residency card is always uncertain about the foundation of living, working, or building a business in a new society when compared to a foreign entrepreneur who is already a naturalized citizen or has family member residency status in that country.

Compare the temporary residency status to naturalized citizenship for a foreign entrepreneur, and you discover that with one, you are in control but have more work to do, meaning you still have stiffer regulations like minimal or no access to loans and grants, while with the other one, you are more in control of your entrepreneurial opportunities.

As a naturalized citizen, you've more likely crossed that line where you can call your new society your home. This takes away more than fifty percent of your residency huddles and gives you an equal opportunity just like every citizen to access loans, grants, work, and travel.

In April 2018, I got a call from a big winery brand for a potential distribution partnership, and part of the negotiations required that I travel to the partner's country for a facility tour and possible discussions. Even though I was a legal resident with family member status, I still could not travel because my residential status does not include the rights to travel to the partner's country. However, with citizenship status, I could simply hop on a plane and seal the deal. I had opportunities to apply for a visa, but my circumstances limited my time, and I wasn't willing to go through the cumbersome visa application process.

In conclusion, various residency status and regulations can affect your chances of building a profitable business in a foreign country. The visual representation below demonstrates your possibilities on a status by status basis.

Fig 1.5 Foreignpreneur® Residency Probabilities

"Always get into new businesses when there are tougher regulations because finding a way around tough regulations means there will always be fewer players in the industry to compete. Most businesses shy away from tough regulated industries."

Chapter Five

Relationships & Family

How to deal with family, friends &

relationships

Dealing with emotions connected to family and building a business is a hard nut to crack, not just because you will literally have no work-life balance, but you will need to reassure your family every time you miss that all important birthday, family dinner or arrive late to an appointment.

Right from the first time you express your feelings to a foreign partner, either a wife or a fiancée, you are immediately building a cultural gap that will need tremendous energy and constant refilling of the understanding bank to have a productive work-life balance.

As a foreign entrepreneur, falling in love and having a meaningful relationship will give you a good sense of purpose to life, but you need to be culturally educated and accommodating of your partner's way of life. You need to understand that certain misunderstandings could simply be culturally distinct.

Do not be quick to brush aside the emotions of your partner over your business; there is no better happiness when the people you love understand why you do what you do. Do not assume they know, always try to create time for family because if you don't, your journey will be filled with emotional instability that will invariably affect the chronicles of your life and business.

Just before you break up from that three-year relationship because you can't understand why your partner cannot support your vision to be the next Steve Jobs, remember that the people you pass when climbing the ladder are the same people you will meet when falling down the ladder.

Family is the most important support to an entrepreneur, and they are the only support that you may ever get if your failure starts to overwhelm you.

I would have sleepless nights for years, getting up at 2 am just to continue writing code and developing business models but would seldom be disconnected from the environment around me. My wife would ask *"Honey, Why are you always awake?"* And I would answer, *"Can't you see, I am trying to build a better life for us?"* And she replies, *"I just want to be happy, and I want you to care for the little time that we share."* At the time, I didn't realize what she meant as I was blindfolded by my vision to become successful by any means necessary, so— most of those words would always go in one ear and out the other.

I never realized how much it meant to have someone that cared; neither did I understand the value of family support until I had my first major setback in my champagne distribution company. I lost millions and had groaning partners on my neck, but when I looked beside me, my wife was there; she never left. My family was vital in getting me out of what would have been a depressed state of mind.

"Wedding ring is the smallest handcuff ever made, so choose your prison mates carefully and sentence yourself wisely."[16]

In building relationship or marriage, try to understand your problem from the emotional side by showing empathy but strive to solve your problem logically. Perhaps your fiancée is not interested in knowing how many deals are on the table, or if you will be buying the family a luxurious apartment in California. Sometimes, they just need your attention and love to make them happy; they're so glad when you're happy because your happiness depends on theirs.

"Remember, your partner will make a better lawyer than your attorney".

You may ask, why not stay single and be in a relationship after you've achieved success? Success is never satisfactory and can never be a guarantee that you will have a good lasting relationship or a happy family because, being successful is a constant state of thought. Every goal is like a block of thought connected in a chain of events. When you accomplish a goal, you unlock a block of thought, and you immediately start thinking of the next goal, and this cycle continues because you are not satisfied with your goal or you feel you can achieve more. However, this will strain your relationship with your family and friends and can plunge you into depression. It would be best if you were satisfied with each block of success; otherwise, your mind will be occupied by an unending block of failure or un-satisfaction.

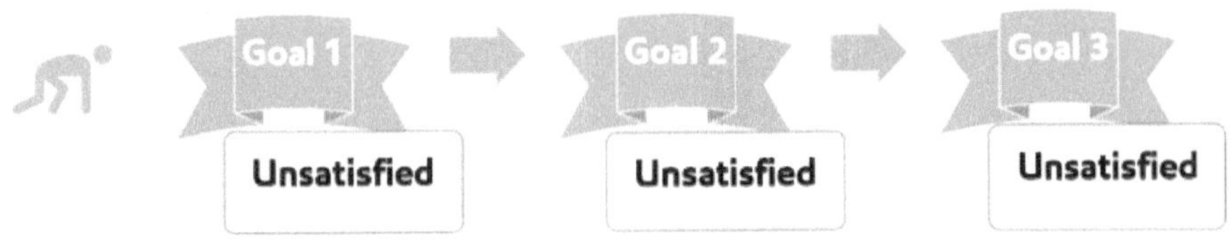

Fig 1.6 Foreignpreneur® Non-Satisfactory Chain Block

The key is to find satisfaction in every goal you achieve and set new goals only if you have the time and energy to accomplish — them.

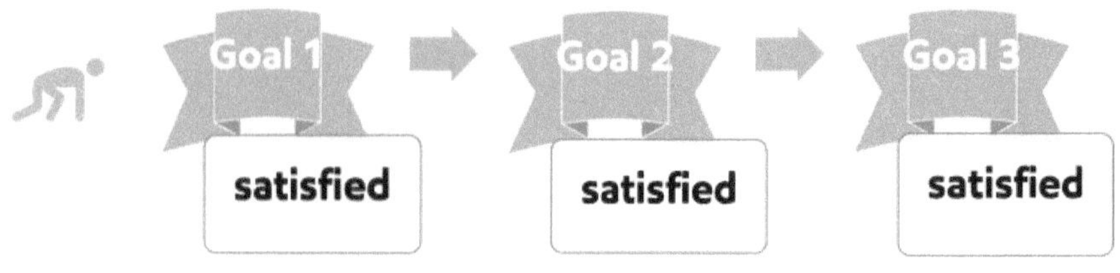

Fig 1.7 Foreignpreneur® Satisfactory Chain Block

Friends or Foes?

You've always wanted to change the world, but none of your friends think you can change the world. In fact, none of your Facebook or Instagram friends have ever shared your business posts. Moreover, you know that peer to peer or word of mouth marketing is the single most significant form of sales. Well worry not because they won't, and you have to get used to this. Probably because, you are naturally a silent competitor to a friend and you are just a regular person until you prove beyond doubt that you deserve to be distinguished. An entrepreneur must first change the people around him or her to see their vision before they can change the world around them because the world is made up of people around you and not the other way round. However, what if the people around you are they ones saying, *"Dave! why are you always acting like you're from another planet?"*

In life, don't expect everybody to like you; for example, I am entirely focused on doing well. I can understand that people are unhappy and criticize but people are quick to go overboard. I accept critics and I don't say it doesn't matter. I prefer it if people say— I am good but I cannot complain when they say I'm not, because I believe:

"Every genius was once a novice and every entrepreneur was once a hustler."

Therefore, dealing with critics as an entrepreneur is never easy, but when those critics are your very own friends and family, it can sting like nothing else. It's essential to address this issue early on if you want to set yourself up for a strong business and personal life.[17]

As a matter of fact, when you launch your business, you naturally think that, at the very least, your friends will be there to support you. So you start your Facebook page, not expecting all two thousand of your "friends" to like it because let's be honest; they aren't really your friends. But you do expect those friends you have met outside the internet to take a second to click that damn thumbs-up button.[20]

"You expect your friends, at the very least, to attempt to change their habits from buying the same products from other stores and instead, purchase them from you. You expect some sort of support. You don't expect people to necessarily go out of their way to help you succeed, but since they know you, you'd think they would want to help you. Well, you're mistaken. "ibid

"What about your closest friends? Those whom you see and socialize with regularly. Those you'd expect would go out of their way to help you with your business and with your dreams? Those people who explicitly told you, promised you, that they would be there to help you if you needed help. Those who you may very well have asked to help you. I'm afraid you can't rely on them, either. They may be supportive in the beginning, but more likely than not, they are just blowing smoke in your face. Friends feel obligated to promise support, but they sometimes never follow through with it. Your oldest friends, your — acquaintances, your colleagues, just about every single person in your life, will disappoint you. Accept this now, and you may have a chance at beating the odds."[21]

In fact many entrepreneurs are so misunderstood that their friends and family don't think they're working,[18] you figure out that you are stuck with friends who think of themselves as working class and categorize you as unemployed just because you work from home, or you are still in the early stages of building your business. They've literally tagged you the insane person, visionless and directionless because of your wild thoughts and unique ideas. They consider you a foreigner of their core beliefs, and this makes you a prisoner of your thoughts to the point of annoyance.

However, why get annoyed when your family or friends do not believe in your vision or dreams? — Let's face it, if you share your new business idea with a family member or your buddy, on that occasion, you shouldn't expect them to grasps everything from the get go, because if they do, then it's probably not a ground-breaking idea, you should maybe consider giving that business idea a second thought. Moreover, the key is not to get worked up with family and friends about your self-acclaimed million-dollar idea. You need to earn their trust and respect through hard work and results. It doesn't matter how great your process is going but how successful you are in the end. Success, of course, has lots of friends, but failure doesn't.

"Lucky are those who have real friends and family in the world of fake people."

When your friends and loved ones don't understand what you do for a living, it can be detrimental to your business in two ways: First, they can unintentionally hinder your goals, either by interfering with your work or repeatedly trying to help you in inappropriate ways. They can also cause you to lose faith in your own business which can lead to feelings of rejection at a time when you need validation the most.[19]

You will need to determine what type of relationship you keep with friends as your first thought when trying to expand your business would be to hire a friend. 1) Because, they are cheaper, and 2) you think it would be fun, you are wrong, the most conscious skill is to cut down your circle of friends to meaningful relationships. The average circle has grown smaller over the years as the level of trust in other people has dropped from seventy-seven percent to thirty-seven percent.[22]

I remember having to work from home with a couple of friends in 2015 when I was preparing for an exhibition of my mobile application in Dublin, Ireland. I would wake up at 3 am to work until noon, and I text my friend to come over, since we were running close to the deadline to get the promotional materials ready. Guess what? Even at noon, my friend was still sleeping. What stood out the most is that I was more passionate about my business. I could hardly scold a friend as that could lead to a break in friendship.

This literally meant I had to put up with a lot of crap since I wasn't paying at the time, and we were only at the ideation stage of the startup business. I learnt the hard way not to hire friends but work with smart and professional individuals who share the same vision as me and are not waiting for me to tell them what to do.

"You don't hire smart people to tell them what to do; you hire smart people to tell you what to do" – Steve Jobs

"With friends, you always need to tell them what to do which will only escalate more tension as they simply see you as a friend and not a boss or business associate. Friends will often associate their work with favors, and they expect you to acknowledge that favor and when you don't, rest assured that you will continue your journey alone. Therefore, find your accountability partner and start looking at fellow entrepreneurs you already know. This may be a friend who owns a business or even someone you met through an online group. Reach out to them directly and float the idea of meeting to talk about business goals."[23]

In the world of entrepreneurs and startups, professional relationships are critical. You can't start a business with friends alone.[24] It would be best if you had business partners, investors, and customers. Make friends from different cultural backgrounds and have more friends in your new society; diversity is a strength; it will give you new ideas.

Consider friendship as a means of building strategic partnerships, pick friends from your new city who can add value to your business and think the same way as you. It is also essential to choose friends from all social classes but only do business with those on the same social level as you as this limits any fall out with friends. A friend who cannot add value to your life will take away the value that you can add to those who matter in your life — through meaningless conversations and arguments.

Avoid getting pulled into the rabbit hole of unnecessary competition with friends because if the only thing you aspire in life is to be better than the other person, then you are not truly free. Do not compete with your friends but create your path, because, friends are meant to help friends and live up to the ethics of friendship. So, avoid making an old friend a foe, and resist the urge to compete without purpose. One thing you've got to understand is; "your competitors can only be king, only on your resignation, you control the circumstances of that resignation". If they want your spot, make them work hard for it.

"The imaginary enemy is the sole reason many people are unhappy; free yourself!"

Even though they may not agree that you inspire them, but they expect you to admire them. So, there's no excuse to engage in a cycle of distraction from self-acclaimed friends. Focus on being good at that which you are good at.

When making friends, be guided by your core principles of friendship. Be careful of the kind of friends that can remove the charger from your five percent low battery to charge their ninety-five battery. They can kill.

Chapter Six

Building Partnerships

The nitty-gritty of communication

Building partnership as a foreign entrepreneur is a very uphill task,

starting with language deficiency, all the way to those sceptical questions of ***"Where are you from?"*** that you get in business meetings.

In some cultures, speaking too much is seen as being arrogant or proud and believe it or not, this may hamper business negotiations and increase your chance of losing out on business deals or even potential partnerships. Understanding culture is key to building alliances; it could be time management, paying for lunch, speaking the local language or merely being kind. Speak to a man in a language he understands[25], and you can get his attention and win his heart.

Dealing with investor pressure or misunderstanding with a potential partner could be the end of a business relationship. There are businesses who've spent years pursuing lawsuits that have hindered the growth of the company.

I am usually not a fan of any form of partnership, but if you must go into partnership, always make sure that you and your potential partner understand the objective of the alliance. Otherwise, you could have important phrases getting lost in translation or even misunderstandings with your prospective partner.

I remember having to spend hours in arguments back and forth with an investor who signed a contract which clearly stated; *"In the event of a loss, we lose together."* Well, when a loss did come, which I never wished for, the investor did not stick to his end of the bargain. His excuse was, *"I did not understand the contract."* It's none of your business if the investor does not understand the contract? I think you should give that a second thought.

There are several factors to consider when coming to terms with a partnership agreement and several practices to follow to keep the partnership on track to ensure that value is being delivered to all involved parties.

The following checklist can guide a foreign entrepreneur when building a partnership:

Fig 1.8 Foreignpreneur® Partnership Checklist

1. *Have a clear-cut direction:*

If you can't say something clearly and directly, wait until you can articulate it to yourself. Talk may be cheap, but it can be worthless if uttered without direction and even cost you a client, a deal, or your whole business.[26]

Make sure that what everybody brings to the table is clear, because there is no guarantee that the value a partner adds to your business at the beginning of the partnership will be the same value going forward. Take, for example, a partner who you've considered a co-founder for two years, and during the first two years of starting the business, that partner was always available to attend meetings, put together presentations and business plans. Fast forward two years later, and the partner no longer makes time and barely attends meetings. However, you are still stuck with a business contract that has given away forty percent of your business to a co-founder who hardly makes time available. These sorts of situations can be avoided with a clear-cut direction and addressed in business partnership by adding contingencies in partnership agreements.

2. *Rebrand yourself for every meeting:*

No matter how successful you are, you won't continue on that golden path if you stop anticipating what's next. Always think ahead because success can quickly inflate egos to the point of isolation.[27]

Rebrand yourself, learn to evolve along with your challenges in life, and only then would all the experiences in life be worth it. You cannot keep giving people the same you for years and expect them not to get bored. You should apply the same principles to your business.

Most people enter into partnerships because they don't feel they have enough value on their own. Be clear on the value you bring to the table. Be honest about why you're interested in creating a partnership. "Why does this relationship benefit my professional and personal growth?" "What do I expect to gain from this partnership?" [28]

Try not to approach every partnership meeting with the same objective or without the flexibility to negotiate your way to a mutual benefit. If you are going into a partnership meeting with a technology company, then try to be conversant with the right technology terms and buzz words to aid your negotiations and be well-informed about trends in the technology industry. This does not mean that you have to be an expert in the field, but it sure will help your potential partner to understand your enthusiasm and knowledge of the business in which you both are about to take a journey.

3. Go for win-win:

You are dominant, you think you are smart; you listen less and talk more because you believe you are the only one that can bring something to the table, or you hold all the incentives in a partnership negotiation. Well, no matter how good you are, there is always someone better. You need to deal with that and understand that in any business meeting, every potential partner is bringing value to the table; otherwise, don't consider partnering in the first instance. Partnerships are simply two people who have what they need, complementing each other. Therefore, strive to control your overzealousness and do not overshadow your partner in conversations. If possible, use —email communication right after your meeting to communicate any other ideas you may have rather than dominate the meeting with only your goal in mind.

You may also want to over promise your potential partner to build trust and confidence during negotiations but this is a No! No. Make sure that you are committing to promises that you can deliver. It is better to under promise and over deliver than to over promise and under deliver. This is the key to building strong business partnerships.

Don't leave that meeting making your host think that you can change the world or create an impression that you're the next Elon Musk. Instead, always let your potential business partner leave the meeting, thinking, ***"I may have just met the next Elon Musk."*** If you are the man or woman for the job, prove it through hard work and results. It is not just those brains that should work well together. Personalities need to get along too.

"More professional connections mean more credibility, more insight into the market and more customer clout. This is the basis for the business axiom — "It's not what you know; it's who you know." Many entrepreneurs will admit that they get almost all of their business through relationships."[29]

4. Stay Calm:

There is no need to hurry into a deal. Sometimes, enthusiasm and excitement can blind you to red flags and foibles. Set a follow-up meeting to address the next steps to make sure that both parties are on-board and of equal commitment.[30] Let's assume that you were going into a difficult negotiation, and you expect your potential partner not to agree immediately to your terms. However, before you knew it, your prospective partner has already agreed to all the terms, and you were left flabbergasted and too excited to analyze the situation. You may have given away all your business advantages to your potential partner.

It could well be that the odds were stacked against you right from the start, and you were not calm enough to understand what your advantages were, and you've just signed off the future of your business to someone you barely knew.

Many entrepreneurs realize late in their journey that they've given away large shares of their business, even before they start making a dollar off their hard work. They were simply too excited to get a seed investment at the early stage of the business. Who could blame them? In their wildest imagination, securing an investment is a dream come true.

"When it is too easy, it's probably a trap or a setup, think again!"

5. *Agree to disagree:*

When hashing out details about what each party brings to the table, expect some push and pull. Many people become uncomfortable with disagreement. Don't stay in a business partnership if you believe it's no longer viable. I've learned that it's better to end the collaboration and regroup than to force something that's not working.[31]

Agree to disagree and do not expect a business partner to agree right from your first sentence. Understand that you have to be convincing enough and give room to accept when you are wrong or when you are not bringing enough value to the table.

Disagreements are widespread in building partnerships with friends based on my personal experience. I don't recommend going into business with individuals, only well-established companies or corporations.

If you must go into a business partnership with an individual, then choose the path of finding a strategic partner. A strategic partner could be any individual or organization that has the same client pool as you. Your shared target market gives ample opportunity for collaboration, and you can learn a tremendous amount by observing their strategies and tactics. You will often be impacted by the same market trends and can have congruent goals. Check in with them regularly and look for opportunities to leverage each other's strengths and successes.

6. *Put it on paper:*

Ever heard of writing it down? Great partnerships require excellent protection. Seal all agreements in writing to avoid messy breakups in the future. This is one of the hardest conversations to have but by far the most important.

How many times have you heard about a partnership that started rosy and blew apart with hard feelings and even costly results? A great way to phrase this is to say, "I'm excited about this partnership, and I think we will achieve great success together. Because I value our relationship so much, let's put our agreement in writing to protect our interests and ensure our growth as partners. How does that sound to you?"

7. *Face to Face Vs. Email:*

You can read the body language of a potential partner or even spot some lies by merely having a face to face meeting rather than emails or phone calls.

Anyone can easily communicate over the internet, but they can hardly fool you face to face. Therefore, when trying to build strong and lasting partnerships, try to make it an in-person meeting over emails or phone calls, especially when you are doing business in a foreign country.

Different countries have different sign languages that could potentially mean in a business meeting context, "This person has nothing to offer" or "I am just standing and waiting for you to finish your jargon." This would save you stress and let you know when to shut up and walk out of the meeting.

While all potential partnership meetings are not expected to end in negativity, face to face can also be good to build a connection over dinner, lunch or breakfast. Wouldn't you love to sign a million-dollar deal over a meal?

8. Time zone:

If making an international phone or video conferencing call, be conscious of the time zone differences and make sure to set a reasonable time for all involved parties to interact.[32]

I know how bad you want to make that phone call after a not so pleasant week on Monday at 6 am your time but consider that it could be nine pm for your business partner.

This seems so easy to figure out, but sometimes, the easiest of items on the checklist often get overlooked, and this is one of them.

When you set up face to face meetings with your potential partner(s), some may prefer discussing business over dinner at seven to eight pm to increase their concentration level, while some may prefer over breakfast, between nine to ten am. I am a morning person and would prefer to have business meetings very early in the morning to start my day and work on quick actionable items.

While it is challenging to tie time zone to culture in the case of a foreign entrepreneur, this simple etiquette can help you get the best out of a partnership meeting.

9. Be in Control:

In inference, one of the essential skills that you may need to build partnerships, secure investments or seal business deals is proper communication skills.

Communication is a significant part of building a business relationship. Your life events and how you react to those events is a critical trait to becoming successful, regardless of any model, book or motivational quotes that you may read.

You walk into a business meeting with an investor seeking funding for your business. You are not aware that morning, the investor's wife just had a baby girl, and in your first exchange of pleasantry, the investor smiles all through the conversation. You keep wondering, what could be making the investor smile? Obviously, it's not your joke as you never intended cracking jokes in a business meeting, because you were nervous from the start.

So, you pull out your PowerPoint presentation, and after making a not so good presentation, you shiver, thinking there was no way the investor was going to invest in your idea after such a poor presentation. However, to your great surprise, the investor replied, *"I am not sure I understand your presentation, but there is something about you that I like."* I want to invest in you.

Jack! You made it, you sealed the deal, doing absolutely nothing but a crazy presentation, you walk out of the meeting excited and, of course, the investor kept to his initial commitment and invested the much-needed capital to fund your business from an idea to a million-dollar company. Your business grows, and you become profitable and even went on to become public, and an IPO would skyrocket you into a billionaire. Forbes came calling, listing you as the richest man in the world by miles.

Now, hold on, let's rewind this life event with a different scenario. Let's assume you walked into that same investor's office, but this time, his wife had just lost a baby, and on your first exchange of pleasantries, the investor neither flinched an eyebrow nor smiled. He ushered you into the office without even offering coffee, and nervously, you pulled out your beautifully designed PowerPoint presentation. Your presentation was excellent; in fact, your performance was that good that you knew there was literally no other way it could be presented better.

However, the investor paid little or no attention because of his family problem and could barely understand your presentation. As a result, the investor responded, ***"I think you made a wonderful presentation, but I don't think I can invest at this time."***

You were devastated. You walloped yourself and wondered how you could have blown a fantastic opportunity to secure an investment, and due to this singular event, you were unable to build your business to a million-dollar company, no IPO and no Forbes list.

Now, before you push yourself into depression, the reason the investor took a chance at the entrepreneur in the first scenario, was connected to the investor's life events and that of the foreign entrepreneur. Sometimes, you don't have to be perfect to be successful, but putting yourself in those positions in life can get you opportunities to achieve your dream.

If you neglect the importance of the reality of the human mind, you would seldom feel disconnected from the reality of being able to manage the dependencies that would make you successful. Applying proper communication skills and seizing important moments in your life and making the best out of them is one of the subconscious traits of a successful entrepreneur.

If you had taken the opportunity to make the moment yours and asked the investor, ***"Hi, you seem sad today?" Is everything okay?***

Let's assume the investor is an open-minded individual and would reply, ***"You know my wife lost a baby, and I am a bit all over the place."*** At that moment, you realize that family is more important than your relationship with that investor. You seize the moment and respond, ***"I think family is important first, and I am fine to come to present another day."*** The investor — replies, ***"Thanks for caring. I am sure your presentation would be great."***

This single act could most certainly change the course of that life event and have you potentially walking out with an investment. As an entrepreneur, your interpersonal and communication skills need to be fine-tuned to realize important moments in your life and how to react to them.

A meeting is an event; a dinner with your wife is an event; a vacation with friends is an event, and a discussion with an investor is also a life event. Your ability to make the best of these moments can directly or indirectly affect your probability to be a successful entrepreneur or a failed entrepreneur.

The visual representation in fig 1.7 explains the interconnectedness between a foreign entrepreneur's life events and the fundamental characteristics that are required to excel.

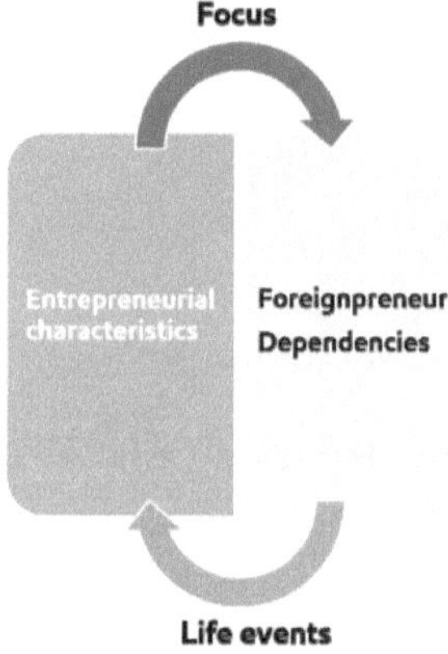

Fig 1.9 Foreignpreneur® Characteristics

A foreign entrepreneur with a unique entrepreneurial trait would always need to manage his or her life events and will require much focus to get through the various challenges that would emanate from those event. Ultimately, the foreign entrepreneur needs to be in control.

Chapter Seven

Culture

Adapt to the new customs and social belief

*L*iving and doing business in a different city involves adopting new ways of thinking. Diversity is the latest trend, and many companies increasingly understand the need to diversify their workforce to bring in new ideas and ways of thinking. For a foreign entrepreneur, adopting new ways of thinking, culture and language of the new city you live in can open your cerebral capacity to create new business models and rebrand your personality to your advantage.

In a globalized economy, cultural sensitivity is essential. Understanding and knowing about cultural differences is a crucial skill for succeeding in business. Understanding language nuances, etiquette, and cultural time management differences can help you navigate many complex interactions. Don't let a deal fall apart due to cultural misunderstandings: Do some research and be open to new cultural experiences and expectations when doing business across borders.[33]

While there are several ways to define culture, put simply, it is a set of common and accepted norms shared by a society. However, in an international business context, what is standard and accepted for a professional from one country could be very different for a colleague from overseas. Recognizing and understanding how culture affects international business in three core areas: communication, etiquette, and organizational hierarchy can help you to avoid misunderstandings with colleagues and clients from abroad and excel in a globalized business environment.[34]

"Customs and etiquette vary wildly from country to country, and business professionals are often unaware of the differences. For instance, the French prefer to shake hands lightly as do the Japanese and South Koreans, and pre-business chit-chat may be customary in Brazil, but this is not the case in Russia, Switzerland, and several other countries."[35]

I remember the days vividly when I would receive an email from a business partner with exclamation marks written at the end of almost every sentence. My cultural background would immediately kick-in to try and interpret the meaning of these type of sentences. I kept trying to figure out the answer to *why in the world would a business partner keep shouting at the end of almost every sentence directed at me in a business email?*

I felt it was unprofessional and lacked courtesy, but I didn't know that these exclamation marks, usually written in this way *"!"* meant that a sentence is important and so I needed to pay attention to the outlined sentence and take urgent action or notice.

However, culture is different across borders. In my country, the exclamation mark is not usually used in this context. Nonetheless, if and when it's used, it meant shouting, screaming or a command.

So apparently, the business partner had offended me without even meaning to, and I took things out of context without knowing either.

Communication skills are evolving as business is increasingly going global and diverse. Therefore, a foreign entrepreneur will need to understand that communication techniques can represent a professional setting without being quick to judge the other partner; otherwise, you run a real risk of your message getting "lost in translation or meaning." For instance, while the Finns [36] may value directness and brevity, professionals from India[37] can be more indirect and nuanced in their communication.

The formality of address is a significant consideration when dealing with colleagues and business partners from different countries, and a foreign entrepreneur will need to understand what form of address works for the city or country they live and do business. Do they prefer titles and surnames or is being on a first-name basis acceptable? While it can vary across organizations, Asian countries such as South Korea, China, and Singapore tend to use formal "Mr. /Ms. Surname," while Americans and Canadians tend to use first names. When in doubt, erring on the side of formality is generally the safest.[38]

The concept of punctuality can also differ between cultures in an international business environment. You may have heard of African time. In 2015, I remember being just five minutes late to a meeting, and the partner simply got up and walked out. I couldn't figure out why five minutes lateness could upset a partner since, in

Africa, you would think that five minutes late is punctual. Even though I had a valid explanation of being caught up in traffic, the partner believed that I should have made plans for transportation and commuted earlier to meet the appointment.

"There are diverse ideas of what constitutes being "on time," and these can often lead to misunderstandings or negative cultural perceptions. For example, where an American may arrive at a meeting a few minutes early, an Italian or Mexican colleague may arrive several minutes — or more — after the scheduled start-time (and still be considered "on time")."[39]

Along with differences in etiquette, come discrepancies in attitude, particularly towards things like workplace confrontation, rules, regulations, and assumed working hours. While some may consider working long hours a sign of commitment and achievement, others may find these extra hours a demonstration of a lack of efficiency or de-prioritization of essential family or personal time.[40]

Eighty-two percent of the respondents to the Deloitte 2016 Global Human Capital Trends survey believe that culture is a potential competitive advantage, and it's very important to business and how organizations recognize cultural differences.[41]

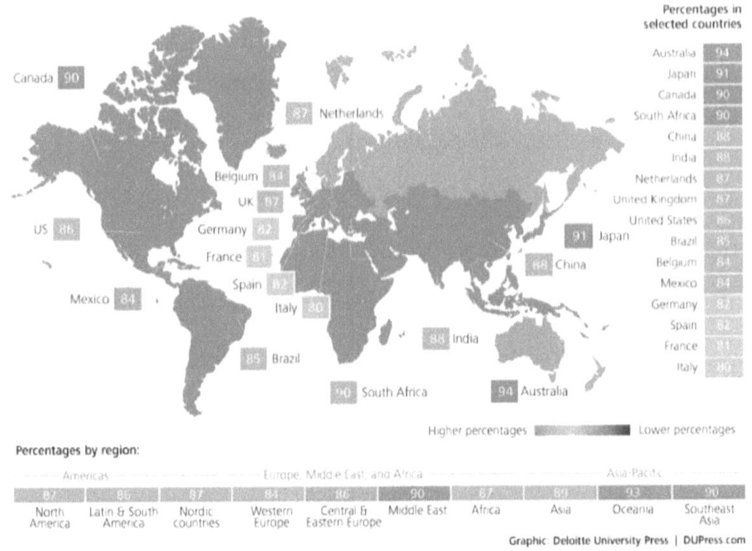

Fig 2.0 Deloitte 2016 Global Human Capital Trends survey

As a foreign entrepreneur, learn to impress with culture, attend meetings with local attire, and when you are given the same opportunity with a local, you must be able to impress more than the local because you must always realize that the odds are still stacked against you.

A peculiar experience for me was in the footballing world when I went for a professional football trial in Slovakia, in 2016. Just like every other player from different countries like Brazil, Ukraine, and the United Kingdom, I believed in my ability to perform well and get offered a professional contract; none of us was willing to give up easily the opportunity to become a pro soccer player. Nonetheless, even though I could dribble pass two-three players, the coach would always expect me to do more as a Nigerian; however, when a Brazilian goes past one player, the coach kept screaming in appreciation; Brazilian-a! Brazilian-a.

Even though I did not and still do not see anything wrong in praising a Brazilian; of course, Brazilians are known to play good football, I felt I was always required to do more to prove myself. I was put out of position by the coach as he perceived that Brazilians are better footballers than most countries in the world. Well, lots of people can argue that, but not when Brazil has won the world cup a record five consecutive times.

Sometimes as a foreign entrepreneur, the odds are stacked against you right from the outset. Do not expect any opportunity to come to you on a gold platter; you need to work two times smarter and harder than your counterparts.

Just like every other dependency that a foreign entrepreneur should be aware of, culture in business could be advantageous from a branding and marketing viewpoint, besides basic etiquette.

When entrepreneurs think of branding, they think of marketing or branding their business. Rebranding your personality is an element of marketing your business that you need to consider, and posting pictures of your dog on social media, how many times a day you ate at an expensive restaurant may turn people of a different culture off. However, it may certainly help you brand your business in an entirely different society where social status is the order of the day.

Some societies even have different types of customers who try to associate a brand to its founder or CEO, and this also reflects in the 2018 facebook.com data breach. Even though the company issued a statement addressing privacy issues, people were still not satisfied with the public announcement. They wanted to hear from Mark Zuckerberg, and investors kept putting pressure on Mark to make a public statement, simply because they know Mark has many followers who are Facebook customers, and these customers or users can relate to Mark's story of Dorm to Dollars. It is important to think of your personality, way of life and how people in your new society will accept your culture; find a meeting point between the two and use it to your advantage.

Chapter Eight

Language

Speak it, use it, you need it

*T*he most important consideration when evaluating a location for a business is the people. In many countries, English[42] is the de facto language of business. However, when interacting with locals in a country that adapts both the English language and the local dialect; it's best to speak the language of the locals. Never forget, when you are in Rome, behave like Romans. It's not just the language you speak; it's how you convey your message that's important.

You can also build connections with your new target audience through learning and speaking the language because a new society means a new target audience.

Daniel, a friend of mine, would always say, *"The Hungarian language is hard and has complex grammar,"* but Daniel has been looking for a job at local businesses in Hungary and could not find a job because most local businesses require the Hungarian language as a pre-requisite. You wouldn't blame them either because the majority of their customers are Hungarians which is a valid position.

On the other hand, Phil, my old-time classmate, is trying to start a Turkish kebab business. Phil has enormous capital, but Phil could not sell a single pack of fried "gyros meal" because Phil could barely understand his customers, who were Turkish.

Now, language is more important to a foreign entrepreneur than capital is to the business in the first instance. This should be one of the essential skills that you need to add to your accolades as a person and not just an entrepreneur looking to build a business.

If you can't speak the language, then you shouldn't be in the business of rendering a service or selling products to the locals of a new city. Perhaps you should try an international business with a global target audience.

It may be challenging to find the time to combine learning a new language and running a business but try to enroll in a language school if possible to help you get familiarized with your new terrain, as well as the essence of the courtesy that you can use when interacting with locals and partners.

For example, the majority of American entrepreneurs view English as the global language and the international language of business. This idea tends to feed the misconception that Americans don't need to invest time and effort in language learning in their education and business strategies. Because of this (in addition to America's geographic isolation), America is a shockingly monolingual nation.[43]

The U.S. Committee on Economic Development (CED) suggests that American businesses lose more than two billion dollars a year to language or cultural misunderstandings.[44]

Consider these statements from the CED:

"For Richard Wagoner, the President and CEO of General Motors, learning Portuguese while on assignment in Brazil increased his effectiveness in working with the Brazilian business community. Douglas Daft, the former chairman and CEO of the Coca-Cola Company, spent nearly three decades living in Asia while working for Coca-Cola. He believes the cultural knowledge he gained from his time in the region shaped his ability to lead the company and considers understanding and valuing other cultures to be an essential skill for anyone working at Coca-Cola."[45]

Nearly eighty percent of business leaders surveyed believe their overall business would increase notably if they had more internationally competent employees on staff, the CED concludes. Additionally, one in five U.S. manufacturing jobs was already tied to exports by 2006, the CED maintains.

In addition to speaking the local language, also having additional language skills can open new doors for you and make the expansion of your business easier, regardless of where you are located.

The British Council *"Languages for the Future"* report pinpoints which languages will be most critical for building international relationships over the coming years, based on trading opportunities and market growth, as follows: Spanish, Arabic, French, Mandarin, German, Portuguese, Italian, Russian, Turkish and Japanese. [46]

"The UK economy is already losing around [fifty billion pounds] a year in lost contracts because of lack of language skills in the workforce." - Baroness Cousins[47]

Apart from just speaking the language, incorporating the language in the various mediums you use in reaching your target market can help to increase your chances of making a profit adversely. For example, advertisements in the local language are crucial, not just to talk to your potential customers in the language they understand but to make it easy for your customers to understand your service and what you do.

I have spent a considerable number of years living in Hungary, and I'm still not fluent enough in Hungarian. I'm better than I was a few years ago when I arrived, but I'm not where I want to be, and this has dramatically impacted my ability to build partnerships. However, my basic phrases and sentences have so far helped me in certain situations to communicate with partners and the locals.

Learning a language is more than just a skill. It gives you freedom. It connects you with new people and to different cultures, you wouldn't otherwise be able to understand. Moreover, according to the Eton Institute, it can even help rewire your brain in a way that improves your memory, amplifies your ability to multitask and strengthens your overall decision-making skills. Lucky for us, learning a language has become more accessible than ever. There are multitude of language apps that can help you achieve proficiency and even fluency.[48]

Chapter Nine

Financing Your Business

Money mistakes may be irreversible

*F*inance is a crucial aspect of your business. You can dream all you want about being the next Jeff Bezos, CEO of Amazon, but without capital, you cannot scale your business from an idea to a profitable company.

What makes this dependency even more crucial is your limited access to grants and loans as a foreign entrepreneur. This means you have to start by sourcing the capital to grow your business yourself; self-funding will be critical in the early stages of your business.

Although many countries do have programs to inject capital directly into the hands of ordinary citizens through state-run venture capitals (VCs) or become a significant limited partner in private funds, a foreigner will have limited access to this loan and grants. This is due to documentation such as the legal residency category and segregation of citizenship rights from a foreigner who is an entrepreneur.

I remember vividly visiting most banks seeking a loan to invest in my business. I was always greeted with the phrase "Are you a citizen?" "Sorry, we only offer loans to citizens." Regardless of whether you are a "Family member of a national," you are systematically excluded as a foreign entrepreneur from access to funding from most local banks.

At one point, a bank official directly said to me, "Sorry we do not invest in foreign businesses" without giving me an option to explain the business model. This regulation may be applicable to most countries and may slightly differ, but the truth remains that most entrepreneurs see their bank as the first point of help in funding their business. If a bank you've banked with for years tells you that "We can't offer you a loan because you are a foreigner" certainly looks like a systematic rip-off. It simply means that it's okay for your money to stay in our bank as a foreigner, but we cannot support your business as a foreigner.

You will need to come up with secondary plans to fund your business, and although some of these strategies may vary country by country, there are common points where similarities are shared and applied.

The following guide can help shape your mindset on possible ways to source funds.

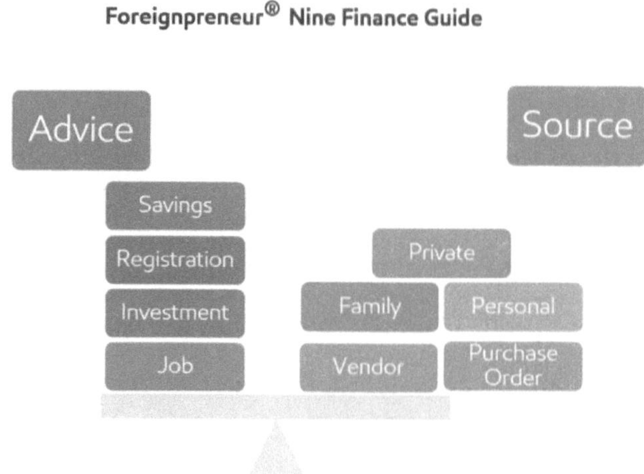

Fig 2.1 Foreignpreneur® Nine Finance Guide

1. Fund your business through savings

Start by saving a few bucks and cutting down on a few things you buy to impress the people that don't care. Top that off with a job; it doesn't matter if you land your dream job or not. However, any job that can pay the bills can help you keep a steady stream of income. A true entrepreneur never has one source of income; they create multiple streams of income to ensure financial stability. I started my first company, Goziex Technologies Limited with less than fifty euros from the savings I had from the mandatory national youth service of my country, Nigeria.

It doesn't seem like much at the time, but it helped sort out a few things like name search for the business and creating a prototype. With the advancement of the digital era, where almost every service is in the cloud, you could get your prototype and proof of concept ready in the shortest possible time if your business is in the technology space, and your basic needs are available.

Limit your expectation of landing a hundred-thousand-euro investment for just a proof of concept. Frankly, if you were an investor, would you consider investing one hundred thousand euros in a proof of concept that is yet to validate its market? I bet you wouldn't and not many investors would either.

2. Start as an Individual and not a Limited Liability Company (LLC)

Start your business as an individual before registering an LLC. This will give you a head start and reduce your tax burden. If your business is yet to make a profit, what is the guarantee that ten to thirty percent of the average tax rate will not plunge you into debt and crash your balance sheet?

"Scale according to your profit and don't scale according to your drive."

Be realistic; there are categories of business registration in almost every country in the world where you can register your business as a sole proprietor. This means you are an individual, and you render your services as one and not a company limited by shares with a board of directors.

Whilst having the *chief executive officer* (CEO) tag can be quite satisfying, having the label at the expense of your business doesn't make any bit of sense if you join the list of failed entrepreneurs, simply because you decided to scale your business when you could hardly pay your gas or electricity bills.

In addition, the cost of registering a business as an individual is way cheaper when compared to the cost of registering a limited liability company (LLC). With this type of business, you give yourself enough room for proof of concept while mitigating the risk of defaulting on taxation.

"If an opportunity exists, take it, don't try to be a superhero."

3. Avoid early investment if you can

One of the most overlooked startup finance unwritten rule is seeking initial financial investment. As important as it is to the existential success of your business, startup entrepreneurs must learn to avoid early investment. Early investment may be the sole reason why a startup business can fail because it exposes the entrepreneur to the immediate uncertainty of satisfying investors rather than customers.

As crucial as it is to seek investment in the early stages of your business, keep in mind that this is a two-edged sword. You may argue that choosing an angel investor is the quickest way to get funding since angel investors are known for investing seed capital in early-stage startups. However, this could quickly have you under much pressure to pay out the return on investment (ROI) and satisfy your investors, rather than spending valuable time building a great product or service that your customers need.

An investor is not your friend but a business partner who wants to make a profit. No matter how many smiles you exchange on a Skype conference call or share a video of your favorite cat, always stick to the script and focus on attaining profitability to keep your investors happy.

Having a prudent finance management skills is important at the early stages of your business. I prefer starting with minimal funding. Most businesses that are built with a large amount of financing in the early stage stand a higher risk of losing connection with the customers as they begin to satisfy investors rather than customers.

You discover that more money gets pumped into promotions or advertorials, why not? Because there is more cash to throw around. However, on the other hand, think about a business that was started from a garage or a dorm room with minimal capital, where every penny counts. That business will strive to find new ways to be profitable while building a great product rather than spending significant capital on promotions or having more leverage to try out every idea "Mr. Marketing Manager" came up with at the coffee break.

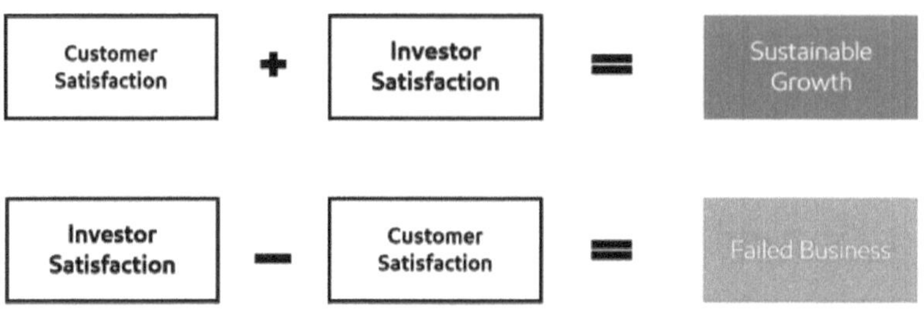

* Without customers, you can't earn

The validation of your idea and generating of revenue is one of the key indicators that you need to watch out for before seeking funding. If your business cannot generate the amount you are asking from an investment standpoint, maybe you should consider not aiming for investment but strive to build a product or service that generates revenue before seeking finance. It will give you some protection from legal and psychological tussles should anything go wrong.

The truth is that not every business needs an investor; some businesses are just about okay as a sole proprietorship or a private company. It's fine sometimes not to seek an IPO too early. Take your time and understand what you have built or trying to create.

In 2018, Elon Musk, Tesla CEO, tweeted, "I am considering taking Tesla private"[49] after being listed on the stock market for years. To some pundits and the court of public opinion, Elon's tweet came as a surprise. They could not understand what would make a billion-dollar company consider going private when thousands of startups dream of being listed on the stock market.

Maybe the question we should all be asking is, *"why did Tesla consider going private?"* It's simple; the sheer amount —of criticism, regulations and investor tantrums that Elon and Tesla face weekly will affect the company's focus on building great products. Elon, of course, realizes this, but to many people, it could be a stupid move.

This is not to say that going public or seeking early investment ultimately insinuates a negative connotation of success, but an entrepreneur should be analytical enough in deciding when to seek financing or do an IPO. If you are not making in revenue at least, a large percent of the investment amount you are seeking as net profit, then it's time to think again about taking that investment.

"Seek investment for expansion rather than for operational cost."

If the reason for asking for investment is to add more staff to payroll, open an office in a high suburb area in the city center over investment to fulfill a purchase order or increase production, then, what you're literally saying is, *"I am willing to risk my entire company."*

In May 2016, when my mobile app company was selected for an accelerator program, I was able to pitch my idea in a boot camp in front of serial investors with a broad portfolio, but one thing stood out when I read the contract for investment possibility. It said, "Convertible Loan" of seventy thousand euros. At the time, this amount of capital would significantly boost my marketing and hire a few employees, but in my personal opinion, a "Convertible Loan" was a plain rip off of an entrepreneur. It was a double edged sword as it grossly read; "If your company fails to become profitable, you will have to pay back the seventy thousand euros with an interest rate, in addition to a service fee that will be deducted at the time of transferring the loan to your company. Moreover, should your company become profitable, then the loan will automatically be converted to equity of ten percent." What a load of jargon.

On a second interpretation, this means, if you win, we win together. If you fail, you fail alone, but before you fail, you have to give us back our money with interest. An entrepreneur must learn where his loyalty lies, either with an investor or the customers.

Without the seventy-thousand-euro investment, I was still able to build a great product that my customers loved and were willing to pay for. Sometimes, startup entrepreneurs do not need validation from investors. There have been known cases of experienced investors getting their prediction wrong on startups who have gone on to become billion-dollar companies.

"Many have 'Gold' but prefer 'Bronze' because the heartaches and responsibilities that come with keeping their 'Gold' can be used to keep that 'Bronze' forever. There's no guarantee their 'Gold' will last, but at least they've realized that they can keep their Bronze forever."

So, before you start having sleepless nights because an investor had just said to you that your idea is bull crap of onion potatoes, think again. Are you building a company or are you solving a problem? If you are solving a problem, there will always be people willing to pay for your product. Not every business needs an investor, so keep that bronze forever.

4. Get a job or have a source of income

For a foreign entrepreneur, financial stability is a very important dependency that requires self-discipline. It may be handy to legally work in a new country to establish connections, build trust, credibility and understand how the big players in the new society are connecting with your new target audience.

There are many jobs out there with flexible working hours that can allow you to become an entrepreneur and an employee. As crazy as that sounds, it actually works, so long as you do not have a conflict of interest with your employer, or you do not use the time meant for your employer to work on your personal business. There are also a couple of freelance jobs available.

"Never trade a stable income for an idea or revenue, instead, trade a stable income for profit."

In 2015, my mobile application software business was selected to exhibit at the web summit in Dublin Ireland, a world technology event with thousands of participants, including investors and tech founders, but a straightforward thing stood out. I was a foreigner with no team, a brilliant business idea, and a malfunctioning prototype.

Who would bet a million-dollar on a foreigner? Before you start thinking, how politically correct should that sound? Try to lend a family member a million dollars. How hard is that? For most investors, whether angel or venture capitalists (VCs), investing in an individual is a proven practice. Even if you do not have a proper team but have an excellent idea, you may still get funding.

Nonetheless, not getting funding is not solely because you are a foreigner, but people like to put their money where they are comfortable. You will need first to have a proven track record and a talented team to stand a chance of convincing an investor.

How do you get finance then, you say? Well, start by finding a job and looking for free resources on the internet to start your business. This has been made easier with the advancements in technology. Today, starting a business is way cheaper than it was five to ten years ago, and the cost keep getting smaller.

Setting up a website yourself today, costs less than twenty dollars per month. You can grab a quick template or use some self-service portals. A job which pays somewhere between three to five hundred dollars per month can get you started.

While you make sense of this possibility, be prepared to pay bills; gas, water, electricity and even internet. Saving to build a viable business is already a humongous task.

Getting water bills in the mailbox was like paying for the most common commodity in Africa, even though a large percentage of the African community is without clean water. However, for those parts of Africa where water is available, we rarely pay monthly fees. Water is sourced from underneath the earth, purified and distributed across homes. Most families have a private water system.

5. Private financing

A quick alternative to funding is to self-finance your business from the start before seeking investment. If you do not have enough money in your bank account, or your piggy bank is rusty; you can make use of crowdfunding as an alternative to angel investors and VCs. Crowdfunding platforms will validate your idea and give you the time to build your unique idea into a business; early investments may strangulate your business due to investor pressure.

This does not mean you should turn down every potential investor. However, if you have an alternative source, then it's preferable to avoid unnecessary early external investments to make sure you understand the business you're trying to build.

6. Personal credit lines

Personal loans or credit. On the one hand, it can also help an entrepreneur to validate a business idea or inject capital into a business. Nonetheless, seek professional advice on what type of loan to apply and which amount is suitable.

The purpose for which the loan was applied for must be clear and used to expand the business and not vacations in Hawaii. When that vacation ends, you may be faced with the reality of paying back a loan which has added no value to your business.

7. Family and friends

If your family or friends cannot lend you a few thousand to try out your new business idea, either you are having a hard time convincing them, or your idea may not be worth a dollar.

Family and friends are a quick source of initial capital for an entrepreneur with little or no pressure required to make a profit. Most families will support, but there are still friends and families who may not be willing to risk their savings.

Explore this alternative source of funding if you have a good relationship with friends or family willing to support.

8. Vendor financing

If you need actual products for inventory, many manufacturers and distributors can be convinced to defer your payment until you sell the goods. This is known as vendor financing. However, many vendors may consider your credibility before financing your business. This type of financing can be suitable for a product distribution business.

9. Purchase order financing

The most common scaling problem faced by startups is the inability to accept a sizeable new order since they don't have the cash to build and deliver the product. With purchase order financing, an entrepreneur can generate upfront capital to operationalize the business. For example, your business deals with the sales of new-fashioned clothes. You have a pending order of twenty thousand pieces, and you only have available capital to fulfill ten thousand pieces of the twenty. However, your customer decides to pay you an upfront payment to produce the entire twenty pieces.

This type of funding helps the business to scale a lot quicker without seeking external investment, and at the same time, it shows that you have a product that is in demand.

Chapter Ten

Conclusion

Pick What You Can

*W*hile I am still trying to figure out why I decided to share my story, what is clear is that there are people out there who prefer to learn from experience than models and sophisticated techniques. The reason I have written this book in plain everyday language is to make sure that everyone, regardless of background, race or religion, understands the traits and dependencies you need to be successful.

When you have the capital for your business but emotionally downed by a family drama, you are likely to lose focus and fail. When you start a business without educating yourself about the laws and regulations of your new location, you are more likely to face a legal case than building a successful business. When you pick a wrong location that is competitive but you have a good business idea, that idea may remain a dream. When you employ friends who don't see your vision, and you build a team around them, you most likely will argue more than making successful sales. When you have limited rights due to documentation, you are more likely to miss business opportunities and controlled access to grants and loans.

Wiggling your way through and managing these dependencies of your success, can shape your entrepreneurship future more than having a twenty slide PowerPoint presentation filled with business proposals and ideas.

Success is never late and can never be late, regardless of when it is achieved. Some will stumble on their life's success at teenage age, some at adulthood, some at thirty years of age, some between forty and fifty, others perhaps at age ninety.

Whenever your success comes, appreciate and celebrate it, there's no hurry to hit success at a young age, while saying "that's the best age to become successful" its all fantasies. Success is even more fulfilling at old age. Some individuals who stumble upon success too early usually don't end up successful or fulfilled at old age. However, some who suffered while young, do end up living the best life at old age. So, don't compare your life to anybody's. Carve your own path, follow your life's timing, and strive to be the best in whatever you do, then allow time and fate to decide the rest.

If your mind is not set out to deliver a minimum viable product[50], you may slip into a rabbit hole desire to change the world. While there is nothing terrible in changing the world, you can quickly get overworked because you've delegated your mind to other challenges such as picking a country, ideation, culture, building partnerships, relationship, family, funding, legal status, and regulations.

Your minimum viable product (MVP)[ibid] or minimum viable service (MVS) needs to be in harmony with your minimum viable mindset (MVM); this will enable you to set realistic goals in the shortest time possible.

To achieve success as a foreign entrepreneur, you must learn to deliver value in chunks, bit by bit. This will buy you time to balance your knowledge of the new city or society. So don't be too be quick to deliver and also quick to become extinct.

In 2015, my wife and I attended a technology event as exhibitors. Five years later, we participated in a world wine event as investors. The motivation to achieve any goal in life is to completely and utterly forget that you ever knew that you couldn't realize it. There is no "super model" or a quick way to success. Books and inspirational quotes can only motivate, but you need to question the norms and the old ways of doing things.

You may remember this famous Aesop's quote:

"Slow and steady wins the race [?]"

What then, are your probabilities in a hundred meters race? Would you still have the edge over your competitors while on a slow and steady pace? Ask questions, be curious, do not just accept norms, find out why they exist, by whom? Moreover, how they arrived at the result?

I do not believe that only reading **books, concepts, and motivational quotes** will make you a successful entrepreneur. I think creating your path and asking the **"Why"** questions, the **"How"** of already existing processes and norms will open the door for you to understand how to solve your unique challenges. I used to have friends who spent hours reading motivational quotes that are not related to the reality of their challenges. "Never give up, but what's the plan?" However;

"Just as our names are different, so are our struggles."

"The patient dog eats the fattest bone."— (African Proverb) What happens when there are five dogs, and only one bone. Will you still be patient? You need to figure out answers to questions like, Do I need a loan to start my business? Do I need to commit to a long term relationship? Can I cope with the way of life and social beliefs of my new society? What legal documentation will be a roadblock to my ambition? If these questions do not have answers, you are leaving yourself vulnerable to uncontrolled— life events that can end your journey to building a profitable business. Having an answer to one is not enough; you need to have answers to all of them.

You may sometimes be lucky to scale through and become successful without being aware of these dependencies, but that does not mean they don't exist. It could well be that you didn't notice, took care of them or were lucky to have them work in your favour, but an entrepreneur does not have to base his or her business on luck. Being successful is a result of hard work and careful planning.

If an entrepreneur starts a business hoping to get lucky, when failure surfaces, there is a likelihood that the entrepreneur will find it difficult to bounce back because the foundation of your business was built on luck.

Even if you lose ten million dollars made through hard work, the chance is that you can remake another ten million by applying the same strategy as the previous. Now, compare that to making it back, if you made it through luck.

"A bird sitting on a tree is never afraid of the branch breaking because its trust is not on the branch, but its wings." - *Charlie Wardle*[51]

Just because it didn't work out doesn't mean it wasn't a necessary part of your journey to becoming whom you're meant to be. As an entrepreneur, there are essential attributes that you should have. These attributes are in the DNA of almost every successful entrepreneur. I have grouped them into two; **"Personal"** and **"Managerial,"** which I consider effective based on my own experience.

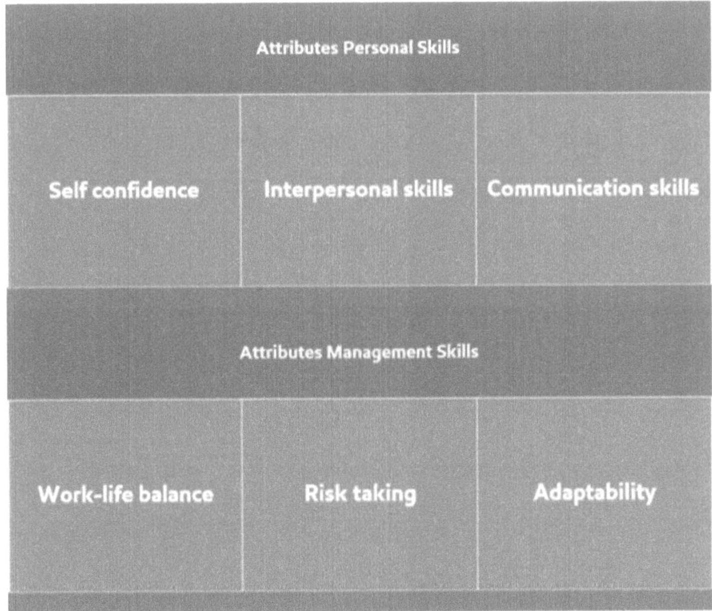

Fig 2.2 Foreignpreneur® Attributes

- **Adaptability**

Many times I've been fortunate to cross the path of people who crack under pressure. Their inability to adapt to a new challenge is evident in their agony and cries of an unjust society. The mentality that society owes you justice will only complicate an already challenging situation. Take responsibility for your challenges and figure out new strategies to solve your problems or adapt to your unique situation.

"If you can't control the situation, adapt to it."

I had just received a call from my port clearing agent that over ten thousand bottles of champagne had accumulated millions of naira in demurrage. The National Agency for Food and Drug Administration of Nigeria had requested additional certification paper for distribution and at the same time, the government has increased the value added tax (VAT), levy and custom tariffs simultaneously.

The Nigerian laws change by the second and neither did I anticipate how difficult making an international shipment to Nigeria would be. I thought shipping would be as easy as loading the container on to the trucks, submit a few documents and voila! Off you go, but I was wrong. Not only was I on the verge of falling into depression, but I also had my phone ringing every —minute. "Davies, you promised that you could handle everything?" My partners fumed.

I had nowhere to hide but lying down on my bed all day, thinking about "How in the bull crap of onion potatoes did I get here?" It was more comfortable than sitting in the doctor's office running diagnostics that returned symptoms of stress. "Davies, you need rest," the Doctors say, "There's nothing wrong with you." I will go home, and my chest would pound every time I get a phone notification. "Could it be the port clearing agent?"

As a Nigerian, who owns and operates businesses in Nigeria, I can tell you that, doing business in Nigeria is a very uphill task filled with bureaucracies, multiple taxation, outdated and stringent business laws. Developing countries are poorer not because of their geographies, cultures, or because their leaders do not know which policies will enrich their citizens but because of enacted policies and theories that don't work.

A country where moonlight is still regarded as an alternative source of light when making small scale transaction on the busy suburbs of major cities, for relatively maximum hours of the day. The citizens of Nigeria have every right to criticize the government. However, I still found a way to adapt and thrive in the Nigeria business environment. The difference between how it works and how it is used is simply how it is understood.

An entrepreneur needs to adapt. Some situations are temporary. I realized that the situation I have found myself in, is one which determines the future of the business, I had to adapt to the new situation by rethinking my approach to doing business in Nigeria. I had to source all needed documentation on time, do proper research to keep myself up to date with the ever-changing Nigerian laws. I incorporated contingencies and unforeseen circumstances in my model and saw it as part of doing business in Nigeria and what to expect. I could have given up, but I choose to adapt.

"Every day new challenges? New challenges, new strategy!"

Don't be easily discouraged either. Pick yourself up because you are as good as your last failure. When you solve a problem or get through the challenges of your negligence, it becomes knowledge. Like I previously mentioned, there are no secrets to success. It is the result of preparation, hard work, learning from experience, and a little bit of common sense.

"Because you'd rather be "Too focused not to be confused." Or "Too confused, not to be focused."

- **Risk Taking**

How many times have you failed? Looked for that glimpse of hope that your decision was right? Risk, as defined by the "Business Dictionary of Finance": is the probability that an actual return on an investment will be lower than the expected return. Financial risk is divided into the following categories: Basic risk, Capital risk, Country risk, Default risk, Delivery risk, Economic risk, Exchange rate risk, Interest rate risk, Liquidity risk, Operations risk, Payment system risk, Political risk, Refinancing risk, Reinvestment risk, Settlement risk, Sovereign risk, and underwriting risk.[52]

If you flip the pages of most entrepreneurial books and models, they all motivate you to take the risk, the bigger the risk, the larger the reward? However, while I agree that risk taking is part of leaving your comfort zone to actualize your business plan. If and when you have an opportunity to avoid risk, take that opportunity. Don't try to be a superhero; it's common sense to separate bad from good.

There are many entrepreneurs who don't know when to stop; they are too motivated to see the red flags. Why stop? Because you think you've failed. Calculated risk is a good entrepreneurial trait, but taking uncalculated risk is an attribute of an entrepreneur who exposes his or her business to failure.

I remember vividly, waking up and staring at my email notifications. "We were unable to charge your card" it read. Each time I get these messages, I never seem to realize that I was paying for various marketing tools instead of perfecting my business model. I was over marketing and at the same time taking a risk in investing in a business model that was not working. My ego did not let me accept the fact that I need to go back to the drawing board to figure out how to build a great product.

I was not generating revenue; neither was I profitable but I was running on a negative balance sheet with the belief that someday I was going to get that one paying customer.

The turning point came when I focused on customer satisfaction and took my time to build a great product. First, I cancelled all the automatic payments to advertising platforms and automated marketing tools and embarked on extensive user research to find out what the users want to see on my mobile app.

At the time, I was developing more of the travel services, such as airport taxi, accommodation and flight but I missed the fact that, a university student would only consider booking a taxi service, If and only when they'd secured an admission. My research proved me wrong, so I switched from focusing on travel services and focused on creating a great user experience for the students.

The result was thousands of download on the Google Play and Apple store combined. More students were using the app, like never before in the history of its development.

However, this success, I did not attribute to just changing the model, but to my ability to confront my reality-check and accept that I was taking an uncalculated risk by leaving my entire business to luck. This meant hoping that the app downloads and engagement will grow organically without realizing that I was over marketing without a user focus. My ability to have a plan "B" when I recognized that plan "A" was not working, is what I acknowledge as a valuable attribute of an entrepreneur who takes a calculated risk.

It's fantastic when plan "A" works, but what happens when plan "A" fails? Having a "B" plan is not an option; it's a must-have. It's probably the most sought after risk management plan for sustaining a business. In today's world, this is regarded as being innovative, but in more precise terms, it simply means:

" Do not put all your eggs in one basket."— Miguel de Cervantes (1615)

Don't assume that everything will go as planned; or be blinded by your drive to be successful more than the factors that need to correlate to make you achieve your objective.

Avoid the do it all syndrome. Let's assume Michael, a friend of yours, is a successful bank executive, and you always wanted to be like Michael and be a bank executive. Two weeks later, you discover that Stephen, an old classmate of yours, has built a profitable online store, and all of a sudden, you want to own an online store as well. You have the skills to become a tennis star, a singer or even a politician, yet you never seem to figure out which one of them you need to do. Evaluate your skills, time, commitment and dependencies and focus on building a business in which you have all the pre-requisite skills.

If you realize at the point of failure that you probably needed to be aware of other factors, you may never get the opportunity again in life because the life events that have brought you to the point of realization will be different next time you take the same journey. Always see the bigger picture and understand all the factors that will affect you and instead take calculated risks.

Life is the consequence of a series of choices you make. If you make good choices, you won't have a bad experience. If you make bad choices, you can't have a pleasant experience. Take as long as you need to make your decisions. Don't be rushed because you'll live with the consequence.

- **Communication Skills**

One of my favorite attributes is my ability to communicate effectively. However, I didn't develop this skill by paying for a couple of online courses. I learnt it the "Hard way." After losing friends, investors and partners, I started to ask myself "Perhaps, I need to change something about myself" This does not mean that I am a bad communicator, but I discovered that I often over sell my ideas and dreams. You can call it "Over promising," but I call it "Marketing."

"Don't use your mouth to write a check that you can't cash with your hand."

An entrepreneur should have the ability to communicate effectively, — that which is important to his or her business. It could be a business meeting, marketing video, or simple email communication. Always remember that people want to know the answer to the question "What is in it for me?" (WIIFM).

I go on a coffee break with friends, I tell them about my ground-breaking ideas. I start with a monologue of all the challenges I face with the business. It often starts with a high —pitch and then, they reciprocate with an enthusiastic response until it gets boring. They start to ask, "What is in it for me?" and then, it ends with "Good for you."

The truth is that everyone is focused on making their lives better; don't waste people's time with meaningless conversations.

When you get an opportunity to communicate your idea, focus on telling what would be beneficial to your audience. It could be earning money working together on the project, or revenue by investing in the business, whichever one it is, focus on what is in it for me? (WIIFM).

I had times when I have lost investment opportunities because I over communicated the technical aspect of my mobile app and instead of focusing on explaining more of the business aspects, how revenue will be generated and investor's benefit.

In the summer of 2016, I presented for an opportunity to get seed investment for the Study in Europe mobile app. I had on my slides; the financial forecast which showed my projected revenue at one billion euros in three years. Hold on a sec, and I know what you are thinking, "I'm crazy," you're probably right, "I was." I am a software developer, not an accountant. So sometimes, I get my presentation and technical information correct, but the ambiguity in financial details make the investors pass the opportunity. In this scenario, I should had been more realistic with my financial projections, because, let's face it; there was no way in the world — I was going to generate a billion dollars in revenue within a three-year span. Communication is key. Most foreign entrepreneurs fail at effective communication because, they have not imbibed into their communication the cultural differences in unique situations, realistic thoughts or win-win contingencies. The best way to understand this — is to view your responses from the perspective of your potential investor or prospective customer's shoes. If you had that twenty thousand euros in your pocket, would you invest in yourself? and if you did invest in yourself, how long will you be willing to wait, to recuperate your investments?

I have read books which focus on teaching entrepreneurs the persuasive skill. However, what most of these books fail to pinpoint is the reality of complexity in diversity. For example, it may be harder to persuade a Nigerian to buy your product with a simple explanation of the benefits of the product, without giving out incentives like a coupon or gift card, better than selling your product to an American by hiking the price of your product to create an artificial sense of value added. How complex is that?

This is because to communicate effectively; cultural differences can help you finesse your persuasion skill. Rather than keep throwing your darts at one target, how about throwing that dart at many? You were not robbed of the opportunity to learn how from the beginning. It's a choice, if and when you decide to learn a new skill. So spend some time to fine-tune your communication skill.

- **Work-Life Balance**

I never knew what work-life balance meant until my eyes started to hurt. I required medical glasses to aid my vision and my heart palpitations became rhythmic jazz music. I was always dizzy and tired. Skipped breakfast, missed birthdays, late to family dinners and round the clock working. Why should I care? I wanted to be successful by any means necessary.

I read every motivational book and quote that I could lay my hands on. They were a source of inspiration filled with models and words from the acclaimed self-made entrepreneurs. So I was never thinking about failure but only to keep going, even at the expense of my health and family. I had no control over my life events and literally no work life balance. To say the least, I had no clue how to manage time.

Time management skill is a beneficial attribute that an entrepreneur should have if you intend to have a healthy life and work balance. The pendulum can swing back and forth, but with proper time management, a delegation of tasks and not being the only smart person around but learning to teach others to do things the way you do can help you relive some of the efforts required.

I remember being the only developer of the Study in Europe mobile app. I was the founder, CEO, programmer, marketing manager, graphics designer. This meant I was doing things that initially should have been assigned to a team. My time was split, doing multiple roles.

This is not to say, that I did not want it delegated, but at the beginning of the life of the business, I did not have enough capital to hire as many talented people as I'd loved to, most of my friends who were willing to help did not have the pre-requisite skill, which meant having a friend who is good in accounting doing the graphics job or having a friend who is good in design doing the marketing job. The best form of misplaced priorities as I call it. Sometimes a business doesn't fail because of processes but people.

I was at the same time, simultaneously building my champagne distribution business and working for an energy company as an IT professional. On top of all that, I was playing active football in the Hungarian league and being a dad and a husband.

You may have guessed it right at this point, my personal life sucked and my social life suffered. I stopped going to parties, recreational activities or creating family time. These decisions where mine and I make no excuses for them, but I was naive of how to handle time management and at so many crossroads, I had to choose between my personal life and my business. However, I didn't have to stop my business, thanks to having an understanding wife and delegating parts of my tasks to individuals who were talented enough and to teach people around me all I knew about my business and to empower them to make sound decisions.

I started working with a co-developer in 2018 and we both used various collaboration tools to make it easy to manage the mobile app business. My wife and I had an agreement of how much hours on the weekend that I had to give to my book writing, my champagne business and when I have to make myself available for a family event.

We agreed that she makes the plans and I make myself available without excuses. Now, I am not going sell you the illusion that I meet up my end of this agreement all the time, but I have in most cases honored my words and made sure that the time I give to my business does not clash with my family time.

Therefore, you should strive to build an effective work-life balance if you want to live to reap the dividends of your hard work. If you are smart enough to build a business, you should be smart enough to find a balance, dig deeper.

- **Self Confidence**

"You might not be a leader, but you are leading" & "You might not be a looser, but you are losing" the difference is self confidence, without believing in yourself, why should people believe in you? Why will a customer take a chance to purchase your product or service, if you are not confident enough to convince them?

After invading Greece and receiving the submission of other key cities, Phillip II of Macedon sent a message to Sparta: "If I invade Laconia, you will be destroyed, never to rise again." The Spartan ephors replied with a single word: "If."[53]

One of my favorite word is the "If statement." — I apply it in my everyday life and as a software developer, I would say; "A program code is never complete without an "If." statement." Therefore, if and when you feel nervous about a complicated situation, always analyze the ***"What if's ?"*** — This can help you regain your confidence, whether it is an investor who's about to pull out from the business or a partnership that is about to fall apart, be confident to view things from the angle of ***"What Ifs?"***, starting from, what if you were better off not staying back in that complicated partnership in the first place? ***"What If?"*** better opportunities are locking around outside the partnership? Confidence is not just the art of believing in yourself, it includes the ability of the entrepreneur to be analytical enough to answer the "What Ifs" in a logical way.

As much as you need self confidence, there is a thin line between the latter and arrogance. Do not let self confidence get in the way of your success, due to overblown ego and self gratification. You've made your first one-thousand-dollar profit, instead of investing in your personal development, you've decided that you no longer need to learn new marketing strategies, you start to dominate business meetings without letting business partners talk. Why should they? You are the new entrepreneurial genius, so everyone has to hear what the genius has to say.

You are in the middle of closing a million-dollar business partnership. So you head out to the Bahamas for vacation and exhaust almost every money you have. Why shouldn't you? You have it all figured out and confident that the business deal would go through and you will be a million-dollar richer.

However, right in the middle of your vacation, while you are about to pour one more glass of Torley Chardonnay, you get a call that the business deal fell apart. How could this happen, you say? Well, no business deal is one hundred percent guaranteed until you have the contract signed and the money in your bank account. Self gratification and over confidence can be a two-edged sword. On the one hand, it is good to have confidence but don't get lost in the moment that you fail to apply common sense.

When running a hundred-meter race do not stop in the middle of the race to look back at how much distance you've covered, other competitors on the track would overtake you. Reserve your personal gratifications until the end of the race and stay focused on the goal.

If an opportunity exists, take it, don't try to create one. A journey of a thousand miles starts with a step but not the wrong step.

- **Interpersonal Skills**

I remember in 2012, going to the office of a transport company CEO to discuss my idea for the use of *SMS to book* intercity bus ticket. He immediately directed me to discuss the proposal with one of his managers. The manager was in his early twenties. We were probably the same age range, young and passionate as me. However, I discovered that our personalities weren't a match.

The manager started a marathon of questions, asking me the core details of the business and financials. Honestly, I didn't do my homework well and didn't see anything wrong with his questions but I had a problem with his dominant attitude and arrogance.

However, without his acknowledgment, the CEO will not be opening my proposal, which meant my interpersonal skills were on the line. I realized that my relationship with the manager would be an essential part of getting the CEO to review my proposal, so I smiled all through the conversation, answered his questions and even cracked up jokes with him and telling him, how smart I think he is.

This made him feel more important than he already thinks of himself, and we instantly built a connection and this allowed me to present my offer to the CEO.

Now, it is essential to note that the proposal did not pull through but my interpersonal skills gave me the ability to interact with someone who would have been a deal breaker in a potential business opportunity.

Both verbal and non-verbal interpersonal skills are fundamental when it comes to your business. When you can speak to people articulately, you avoid communication errors and more likely to have happy partners and customers. It's just as important to maintain the correct tone of voice as well.

"Non-verbal communication consists of facial expressions, hand gestures and body language. It can also determine whether or not your interaction results in a satisfied customer. When you combine both verbal and non-verbal skills, the result is an authoritative demeanor that may help to determine the success of a company."[54]

"In addition, superb interpersonal skills encompass listening skills, problem-solving, decision-making and negotiation skills. The ability to communicate internally with employees and co-workers is just as important as building and maintaining solid relationships with customers."[55]

When I conclude business meetings, I apply the forty-eight-hour communication rule. "Never let a follow up to a meeting pass the forty-eight-hour mark" this is essential to build trust quickly, show commitment and to let all participants remember the meeting notes vividly.

Now, I know you may want to continue reading, but unfortunately, I will have to stop writing and thank you for reading this far and wish to leave you with a few more sentences; Timing is essential to a business because you may be several years ahead of your time or way behind your time. For example, building a space travel web application in 2019 (Today) seems like a bad idea, but developing the same website in 2060 (Future) could go on to be a successful business. You never know, perhaps humans will already be traveling commercially to space in 2060, and you may be in the business of providing them an easy way to find, book and travel to another planet. If there is no problem, then there is no matching solution and then, "There is no business."

What's hard in a good "sale" is when someone with a problem that needs to be solved, finds someone with a solution. There is one thing stronger than all the models in the world, and that is an idea whose time has come[56], don't be swayed by the fancy tagline of "Become your own boss" that you forget to delegate the capacity of your mind to other factors that would need to come together for you to become successful.

I am not entirely throwing all the success models out there in the trash can. However, I argue that the models are illusionary and devoid of the real challenges of an entrepreneur and more significantly, how they are marketed; persuasive and overdramatic.

If mentors feel an absolute obligation to share the secret to their success (Which I don't believe there is) or give advice, then they should focus on the real-life struggles and factors that made them successful.

I do not live an advice dependent life because the world is opinionated. I only filter what's of value to me and backlog others. If your advice is so good that you want to choke it down people's lives, then use it yourself, so simple.

It's a waste of time and energy to rip yourself apart over something you no longer have the power to change. There are so many positive things you can do with your emotions and energy.

In business and to succeed in life, you will need to make hard decisions and painstakingly back those decisions. Becoming a business founder or an executive is hard, and building one as a foreigner is even harder.

I hope that this book will be valuable to you, a friend or someone you care about.

Appendix A - Exercise

1. Briefly describe two personal business ideas you are trying to scale.

Business "A" description:

____

____

____

____

____

____

____

____

____

____

____

Business "B" description:

____

____

____

____

____

____

____

____

____

____

2. List the skills that may be required for you to achieve
    your goal (e.g. communication skill)

____

____

____

____

____

____

____

____

3. Write down the capital that you have for each of the
    businesses (can be savings or zero capital)

Business "A" capital:

Business "B" capital:

4. On a scale of 1-100 write down in percentage, how
    much passion and energy you think you have, for the
    both ideas.

Business "A" passion and energy (PE):

Business "B" passion and energy (PE):

5. Write down the time in years, that you will need to learn any missing skill or source capital.

Business "A" time to learn (TL):

Business "B" time to learn (TL):

Using the Foreignpreneur ® comparison formula **(Capital/Passion & Energy + Time to Learn – Skill set = Readiness)**, calculate your readiness scale for each of the business idea, and choose which business idea you should scale. (Note: the business idea, whose readiness number is higher, is considered the idea that you should scale. The higher the readiness scale, the more prepared you are)

Business "A" **(C/PE + TL – SS = RE)**:

Business "A" (**C/PE + TL – SS = RE**):

Based on your calculation above, check the box for the business with the highest number of readiness:

Business A

Business B

Appendix B - Disclosures

While I have tried to be as open as I could, sharing my personal stories. I have concealed specific details which may have legal implications. I have deliberately omitted the names of people, places, and things. However, all stories and examples are my real-life situations. The stories are accurate as I can remember at the time of writing.

My lawsuit with the Telecommunication Company is still ongoing. In 2019, I won the case at the federal high court in Nigeria for the infringement on my copyright. This was in regards to my idea for *"Telecommunications mobile recharge card advertisement"* The original damage was for over one million dollars (not exact figures).

I wish to state that the views I expressed in this book are mine and not those of my business partners, family, or company I work for. In completing this book, I read various other publications, research papers, and articles and have on occasions, incorporated these views in my paragraphs. These extracts were referenced appropriately in the bibliography.

I hope that this book achieved its purpose of drawing attention to the mental health of entrepreneurs and not just foreign founders and executives.

Appendix C - Research Results

Question One:

On a scale of 1 -100 how much do you think of "Success", when starting a business?

Answered 56   Skipped 0

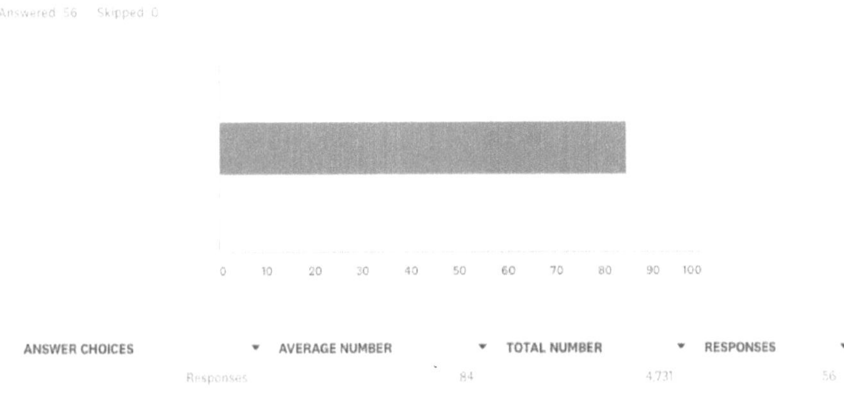

Participants of the survey when asked, how much of success preoccupies their mind before the start of a new business? Fifty-six of the total participants averaged eighty-four percent. This validates my earlier postulation that; the majority of startup founders or individuals who are about to embark on an entrepreneurship escapade, delegate a significant capacity of their mind to success while giving less attention to other factors.

The first question was structured in a way that prevented participants from seeing the content of question two; this provided more in-depth insight on what participants consider as the most critical dependency at first glance.

Question Two:

What are the factors you consider important when starting a business?
*Multiple selection

Answered: 56   Skipped: 0

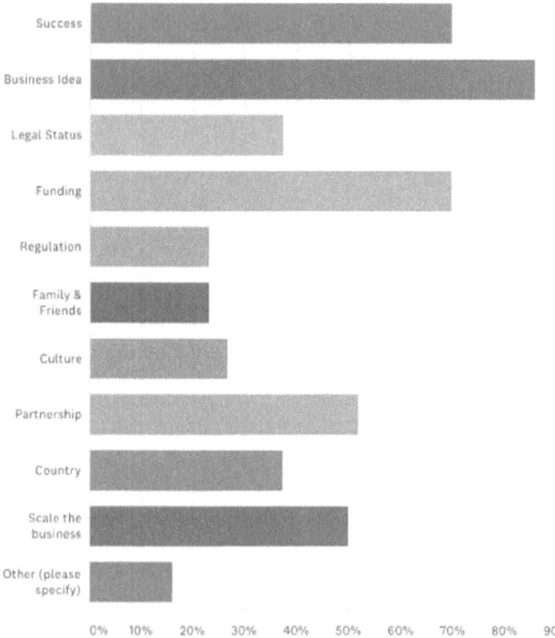

ANSWER CHOICES	RESPONSES	
Success	69.64%	39
Business Idea	85.71%	48
Legal Status	37.50%	21
Funding	69.64%	39
Regulation	23.21%	13
Family & Friends	23.21%	13
Culture	26.79%	15
Partnership	51.79%	29
Country	37.50%	21
Scale the business	50.00%	28
Other (please specify)	16.07%	9

Total Respondents: 56

On completion of question one, I asked the participants to choose, using multiple selection fields, which of the factors they consider necessary to their dream of building a business. I asked them to choose between partnership, scaling the business, country, culture, funding, family & friends, regulation, legal status, business idea and success.

The result showed that the percentage of people who considered success at 84 percent on average, now think that success is less important at 69.64 percent but this drop in percentage can be attributed to showing the participants other factors which they never considered important, when making their choice in question one.

One of the key learnings from the result of the research is the indicator that when most individuals have figured out which business they want to do and have the necessary funding, they fixate their mind almost immediately to how to become successful.

The result also showed that even when participants were presented with other options, none of the participants selected all the factors as important. Again, this shows a lack of understanding that there is no one path to being successful. All of the dependencies are important and should be considered as such.

Every foreign entrepreneur must realize that all of the nine dependencies needs to favor the entrepreneur to provide a solid foundation for a sustainable business. Success is not more important than picking a business idea, so is funding not more important than legal status, because if you have funding and do not have a viable business idea, you're bound to fail and if you have the required financing, business idea, legal stay, family support but you pick a wrong location for your business, failure will be the unsolicited outcome.

Question Three:

Do you own a business?

Answered: 56   Skipped: 0

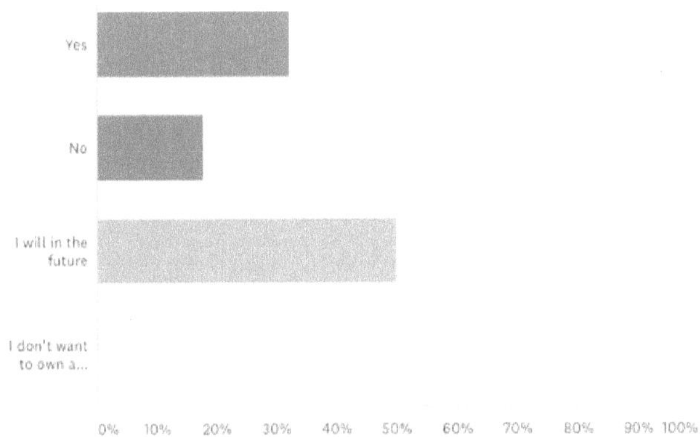

Participants had a diverse background on business ownership; this provides various perspectives to the entire result, which helped conclude that both business owners and non-business owners all consider success more critical than delegating the capacity of their mind to other factors that will lay the foundation for their success.

Appendix D – Referenced Businesses

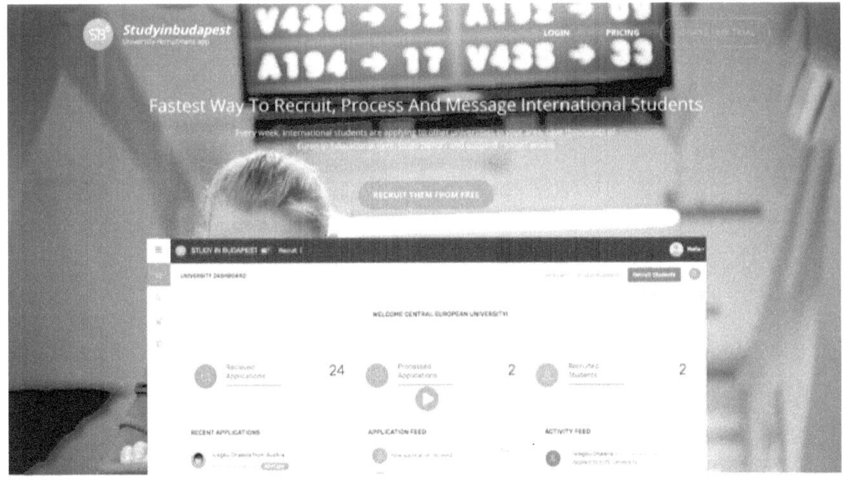

Figure: *Study in Budapest university recruitment app* available at universities.studyinbudapest.com

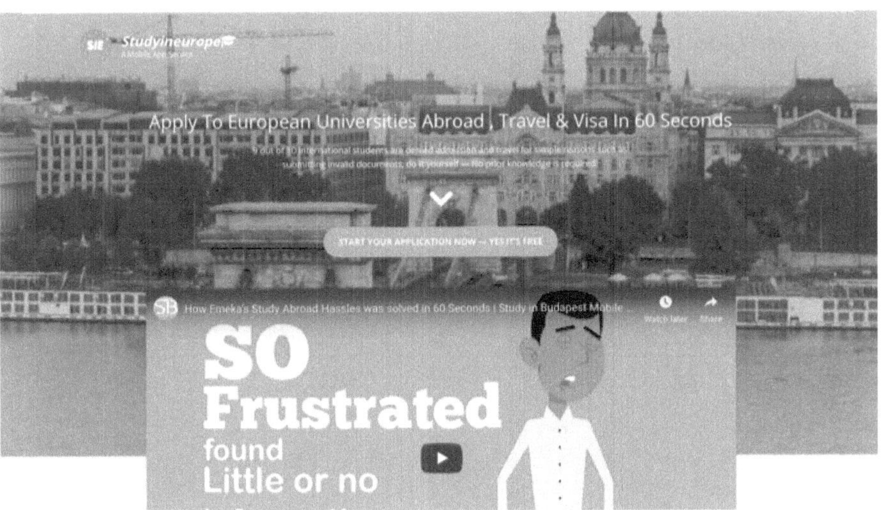

Figure: *Study in Europe admission and travel app* available at www.studyineuropeapp.com

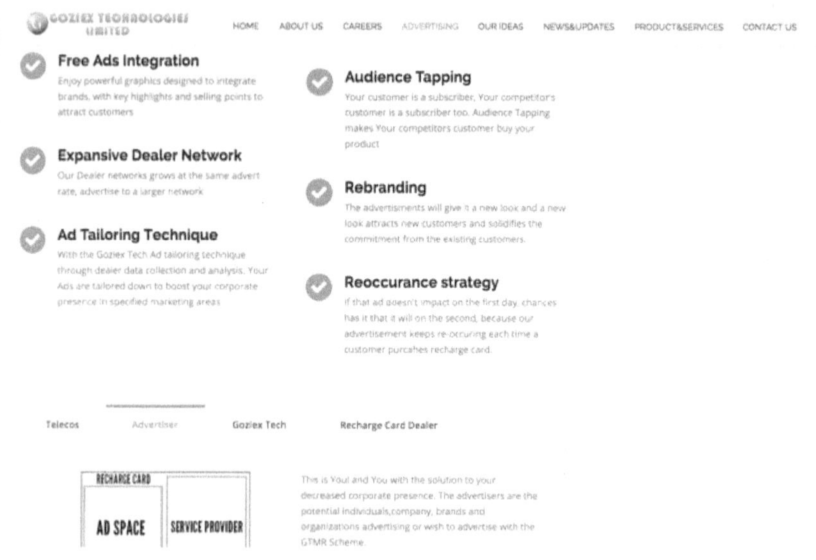

Figure: *Goziex Tech Mobile Recharge Card* available at www.goziextech.com

Figure: *Torley Nigeria wine distribution* available at

www.torley.com.ng

Appendix E – Index

Appendix F – Notes

1. Eric Ries. (2017) "The Startup Way: How Entrepreneurial Management Transforms Culture and Drives Growth". Penguin Random House UK

2. Import Genius. (n.d) "Find New Opportunities in Global Trade". Retrieved from: https://www.importgenius.com

3. Descartes Datamyne. (n.d) "Trade Data Research" Retrieved from: http://www.datamyne.com

4. Laurel Delaney (2013) "Expanding Your Business in New Countries: What You Need to Know" Retrieved from: https://www.mastercardbiz.com/2013/04/10/expanding-your-business-in-new-countries-what-you-need-to-know/

5. "Corporate Tax Rates Around the World" (2018) Tax Foundation. Retrieved from: https://taxfoundation.org/corporate-tax-rates-around-world-2018/

6. "Hey Rumble thoughts on Tesla in China." Retrieved from: https://bwi.forums.rivals.com/threads/hey-rumble-thoughts-on-tesla-in-china/211731/

7. ibid

8. Aaron Labajo (2017) "RE: How did Elon Musk fund his businesses, from PayPal to SpaceX and Tesla? [Blog comment]" Retrieved from: https://www.quora.com/How-did-Elon-Musk-fund-his-businesses-from-PayPal-to-SpaceX-and-Tesla

9. Laurel Delaney (2013) "Expanding Your Business in New Countries: What You Need to Know" Retrieved from: https://www.mastercardbiz.com/2013/04/10/expanding-your-business-in-new-countries-what-you-need-to-know/

10. Medici (2018) "Overview of the Payments Industry: The Ecosystem, Consumer & Wholesale Payments, and the Application of New Technologies: The Evolution of Channels and Means" Retrieved from: https://gomedici.com/overview-of-the-payments-industry/

11. Sandra Wróbel-Konior (n.d) "What Is an E-payment System?" Retrieved from: https://securionpay.com/blog/e-payment-system/

12. Martin Zwilling (2015) "7 Steps for Establishing the Right Business Model" Entrepreneur Europe. Retrieved from: https://www.entrepreneur.com/article/242308

13. Mariah Brown (2019) "How Can Cultural Differences Affect Business Communication?" Hearst Newspapers, LLC. Retrieved from: https://smallbusiness.chron.com/can-cultural-differences-affect-business-communication-5093.html

14. "Launch of Foreign Language Training Programme." (2016). MENA Report, n/a.

15. "Emerging Trends in Real Estate" - Pwc.com. (2018). Retrieved from https://www.pwc.com/gx/en/industries/financial-services/assets/pwc-etre-global-outlook-2018.pdf

16. "A Wedding Ring Is the Smallest Handcuff Ever Made Choose" (n.d.) https://hu.pinterest.com/pin/532832199643406972/

17. Amy Rigby (2007). "The Misunderstood Entrepreneur: How to Crush It Even When Your Friends and Family Don't Get You." Foundr

18. Ibid

19. Ibid

20. Paul Hudson (2014). "No New Friends: Why It's Impossible for Entrepreneurs to Find Real Friends". Elite Daily. Retrieved from: https://www.elitedaily.com/money/entrepreneurship/no-new-friends-why-its-impossible-for-entrepreneurs-to-find-real-friends

21. Ibid

22. Dave, Cohen (2012) "How Far Gone Are We? Decline of the Empire." Retrieved from https://www.declineoftheempire.com/2012/06/how-far-gone-are-we.html

23. Amy Rigby (2007). "The Misunderstood Entrepreneur: How to Crush It Even When Your Friends and Family Don't Get You." Foundr

24. 8 Reasons Why Entrepreneurs Need More Business ... (n.d.). Retrieved from https://www.entrepreneur.com/article/270037

25. "South Africa: Launch of Foreign Language Training Programme." (2016). MENA Report, n/a.

26. Faisal Hoque (2014) "5 Principles for Building Better Partnerships". Fast Company. Retrieved from: https://www.fastcompany.com/3025981/5-principles-for-building-better-partnerships

27. 5 Principles for Building Better Partnerships - Fast Company. (n.d.). Retrieved from https://www.fastcompany.com/3025981/5-principles-for-building-better-partnership

28. How to Create Strategic Partnerships - Opsource Staffing. (n.d.). Retrieved from https://www.opsourcestaffing.com/create-strategic-partnerships/

29. Martin, Zwilling (2016) 8 Reasons Why Entrepreneurs Need More Business Relationships and Fewer Friends. Entrepreneur. Retrieved from: https://www.entrepreneur.com/article/270037

30. Kate Mckay (2014) "How to Create Strategic Partnerships That Are a Win-Win". Entrepreneur Retrieved from: https://www.entrepreneur.com/article/234425

31. How to Create Strategic Partnerships - Opsource Staffing. (n.d.). Retrieved from

https://www.opsourcestaffing.com/create-strategic-partnerships/

32. Target Audience When Launching a Marketing Campaign (n.d.). Retrieved from https://www.coursehero.com/file/pbnpo8/Target-Audience-When-launching-a-marketing-campaign-or-advertising-to-members/

33. How Can Cultural Differences Affect Business Communication (n.d) Retrieved from: https://smallbusiness.chron.com/can-cultural-differences-affect-business-communication-5093.html

34. Katie Reynolds (2017) "How cultural differences impact international business in 2017". Hult International Business School. Retrieved from: https://www.hult.edu/blog/cultural-differences-impact-international-business/

35. CT Business Travel (2015) "Business Etiquette Around the World" Retrieved from: https://www.ctbusinesstravel.co.uk/news/blog/business-etiquette-around-the-world/

36. Expand Finland guide Book (n.d) "Finish Culture & Cross-culture" Retrieved from: https://www.expat-finland.com/living_in_finland/culture.html

37. "Doing Business in India" (n.d). Globe Media Ltd. Retrieved from: www.expatarrivals.com/asia-pacific/india/shipping-and-removals-india

38. "How Cultural Differences Impact International Business" (n.d.). Retrieved from https: //www.hult.edu/blog/cultural-differences-impact-international-business/

39. Ibid

40. ibid

41. Ben Dollar, Marc Kaplan, Veronica Melian, Yves Van Durme, Jungle Wong (2016) "Shape culture: Drive strategy". Deloitte. Retrieved from: https://www2.deloitte.com/insights/us/en/focus/human-capital-trends/2016/impact-of-culture-on-business-strategy.html

42. Jeff (2014) "Why Fluent English Language is Important for Business." EuroTalk. Retrieved from:

http://eurotalk.com/blog/2014/02/19/why-fluent-english-language-is-important-for-business/

43. "How Learning an Additional Language Could Influence Your" (n.d.). Retrieved from https://www.forbes.com/sites/cherylsnappconner/2014/04/17/how-learning-an-additional-language-could-influence-your-business/

44. ibid

45. ibid

46. ibid

47. Lucy Jolin (2014) "Why Language Skills Are Great For Business." Guardian (n.d.). Retrieved from: https://www.theguardian.com/small-business-network/2014/dec/16/language-skills-great-business

48. Mondly Language App Review: Learn A New Language With This (n.d.). Retrieved from https://www.cnn.com/2018/11/19/cnn-underscored/mondly-language-review/index.html

49. Twitter Elon Musk https://twitter.com/elonmusk

50. Ibid

51. "A bird sitting on a tree is never afraid of the branch"
Retrieved from:
https://sites.psu.edu/marissanicolespassionblog/2014/03/2
7/a-bird-sitting-on-a-tree-is-never-afraid-of-the-branch-
breaking-because-her-trust-is-not-on-the-branch-but-on-its-
own-wings-always-believe-in-yourself-unknown/

52. "What is Business Risk" Retrieved from:
http://www.businessdictionary.com/definition/risk.html

53. "Sparta's Response After Philip II of Macedon" Retrieved
from: https://en.wikipedia.org/wiki/Laconic_phrase

54. "How do interpersonal skills influence a business culture?"
Retrieved from:
https://www.investopedia.com/ask/answers/030415/how-
do-interpersonal-skills-influence-business-culture.asp

55. Ibid

56. Joseph Dewey (2015) "Teachings" Retrieved from:
http://www.freeread.com/category/teachings/page/43/